Study Guide

for use with

NELSON

SIXTH CANADIAN EDITION

principles of

macro
economics

MANKIW KNEEBONE McKENZIE

Prepared by PETER FORTURA
ALGONQUIN COLLEGE

and SHAHRAM MANOUCHEHRI
MACEWAN UNIVERSITY

NELSON / EDUCATION

NELSON / E D U C A T I O N

Study Guide
prepared by Peter Fortura and
Shahram Manouchehri

**for use with *Principles of Macroeconomics*,
Sixth Canadian Edition**
by N. Gregory Mankiw, Ronald D. Kneebone,
and Kenneth J. McKenzie

**Vice President, Editorial
Higher Education:**
Anne Williams

Executive Editor:
Amie Plourde

Director of Marketing:
Sean Chamberland

Technical Checker:
Ross Meacher, C.A.

Developmental Editor:
My Editor, Inc.

Content Production Manager:
Jennifer Hare

Copy Editor:
Frances Robinson

Design Director:
Ken Phipps

Managing Designer:
Franca Amore

Cover Design:
Trinh Truong

Cover Image:
Andy Roberts/Getty Image

ISBN-13: 978-0-17-656063-8
ISBN-10: 0-17-656063-7

CONTENTS

PREFACE

Economics is a way of thinking. It provides a tool kit for solving problems and making decisions. You may be tempted to learn economics by simply listening to lectures or relying on common sense. Do not be fooled. Economics cannot be learned by osmosis. Learning requires active participation by the student. This means solving problems and answering questions, then looking at the reasons behind both the correct and the incorrect answers.

This *Study Guide* was written to accompany the sixth Canadian edition of *Principles of Macroeconomics*, by N. Gregory Mankiw, Ronald D. Kneebone, and Kenneth J. McKenzie. It was written with only one audience in mind: you, the student. It is intended to complement the material provided in the text and your instructor's lectures, thereby helping you to be successful in this course.

Objectives of the *Study Guide*

There are three broad objectives to the *Study Guide*. First, it reinforces the text and improves your understanding of the material presented in the text. Second, it provides you with experience in using economic theories and tools to solve actual economic problems—learning by doing! Third, the questions and problems allow you to validate areas of successful learning and to highlight areas needing additional study.

Organization of the *Study Guide*

Each chapter in the *Study Guide* corresponds to a chapter in the sixth Canadian edition of the *Principles of Macroeconomics* text. Each *Study Guide* chapter includes the following sections:

I. *Chapter Overview:* This section begins with a description of the purpose of the chapter and of how the chapter fits into the overall framework of the text. The overview also includes helpful hints to guide the student's intuition in understanding the material.

II. *Self-Testing Challenges:* This section begins with true/false questions and multiple-choice questions. These questions provide useful feedback in preparation for an exam, particularly if the student analyzes the right and wrong answers. Next, there are short-answer questions and practice problems, which provide applications and important extensions of the material in the text. The practice problems are generally multiple-step problems, while each short-answer question is generally based on a single topic in the text. The section ends with an advanced critical thinking problem, which applies the economic reasoning and tools developed in the chapter to a real-world problem.

III. *Solutions:* This section provides answers to all the questions and problems in the *Study Guide*. Explanations are provided for the false responses to the true/false questions.

Use of the *Study Guide*

A study guide is not a substitute for a text. Use this *Study Guide* in conjunction with the *Principles of Macroeconomics* text, not in place of it. How one best uses a study guide is largely a personal matter. Most students will prefer to read through the entire chapter in the text and then work through the *Study Guide*, identifying the areas which need further study and the areas which are already mastered.

Multiple-choice questions tend to be the most commonly used type of exam question. Yet students often encounter difficulties with this type of question because they find that many of the choices differ only slightly. Thus, students should develop and practise strategies for doing multiple-choice questions. The following are some helpful strategies: Read each question and all the choices very carefully—often, only one word is the difference between two of the choices. Eliminate any obviously wrong choices. Mark-up the page with notes, arrows, and diagrams. Remember that the correct answer may not be immediately evident—most questions will require you to analyze numerical and graphical information.

Acknowledgments

We would like to thank Gregory Mankiw for having written such an innovative and lively text, and the Canadian authors for carefully adapting Mankiw's ideas to fit the Canadian experience. Thanks also to David Hakes who wrote the *Principles of Macroeconomics Study Guide* for the U.S. market. His excellent work made producing the Canadian edition a truly enjoyable task.

We also thank executive editor Amie Plourde, consulting editor Rod Banister, and developmental editor Katherine Goodes for their support throughout the process. In particular, we would like to thank Ross Meacher, C.A., the accuracy checker for Nelson Education, without whose sharp eyes and subject awareness our own errors and those unintentionally carried forward in previous editions would not have been corrected.

Finally, we thank all the students who have taken our courses over the years, for it is they who, by their questions, comments, and even frustrations, have enhanced our understanding of economics.

Final Thoughts

Economics can be a tremendously exciting and enjoyable field of study. But it can also be intimidating. We hope that this *Study Guide* will improve your understanding of economics, so that you are able to enjoy the subject as much as we do.

Peter Fortura
Shahram Manouchehri

CHAPTER 1 Ten Principles of Economics

I. Chapter Overview

A. Context and Purpose

Chapter 1 is the first chapter in a three-chapter section that serves as the introduction to the text. Chapter 1 introduces ten fundamental principles on which the study of economics is based. In a broad sense, the rest of the text is an elaboration on these ten principles. Chapter 2 explains how economists approach problems, while Chapter 3 shows how individuals and countries gain from trade.

The purpose of Chapter 1 is to lay out ten economic principles that will serve as building blocks for the rest of the text. The ten principles can be grouped into three categories: how people make decisions, how people interact, and how the economy as a whole works. Throughout the text, references will often be made to these ten principles.

B. Helpful Hints

1. *Place yourself in the story.* Throughout the text, most economic situations will be composed of economic actors: buyers and sellers, borrowers and lenders, firms and workers, and so on. When you are asked to address how any economic actor would respond to economic incentives, place yourself in the story as the buyer or the seller, the borrower or the lender, the producer or the consumer. Do not think of yourself always as the buyer (a natural tendency) or always as the seller. You will find that your role playing will usually produce the right response once you learn to think like an economist—which is the topic of the next chapter.

2. *Trade is not a zero-sum game.* Some people see an exchange in terms of winners and losers. Their reaction to trade is that, after the sale, if the seller is happy, the buyer must be sad because the seller must have taken something from the buyer. That is, they view trade as a *zero-sum game* where what one gains the other must have lost. They fail to see that both parties to a voluntary transaction gain because each party is allowed to specialize in what it can produce most efficiently, and then trade for items that are produced more efficiently by others. Nobody loses, because trade is voluntary. Therefore, a government policy that limits trade reduces the potential gains from trade.

3. *An externality can be positive.* Because the classic example of an externality is pollution, it is easy to think of an externality as a cost that lands on a bystander. However, an externality can be positive in that it can be a benefit that lands on a bystander. For example, education is often cited as a product that emits a positive externality because when your neighbour educates herself, she is likely to be more reasonable, responsible, productive, and politically astute. In short, she is a better neighbour. Positive externalities, just as much as negative externalities, may be a reason for the government to intervene to promote efficiency.

II. Self-Testing Challenges

A. True/False Questions

_____1.   When the government redistributes income by raising income taxes and increasing welfare payments, the economy becomes less equitable.

_____2.   When economists say, "There is no such thing as a free lunch," they mean that all economic decisions involve tradeoffs.

_____3.   Adam Smith's "invisible hand" concept describes how corporate business reaches into the pockets of consumers like an "invisible hand."

_____4.   Rational people systematically and purposefully do the best they can to achieve their objectives.

_____5.   Canada will benefit if we eliminate trade with Bangladesh, because we will be forced to produce more of our own clothes.

_____6.   When a jet flies overhead, the noise it generates is an externality.

_____7.   A tax on beer raises the price of beer and provides an incentive for consumers to drink more.

_____8.   An incentive is something that induces a person to act.

_____9.   Sue is better at cleaning and Bob is better at cooking. It will take fewer hours to eat and clean if Bob specializes in cooking and Sue specializes in cleaning than if they share the household duties evenly.

_____10.   High and persistent inflation is caused by moderate growth in the quantity of money in the economy.

_____11.   In the short run, a reduction in inflation tends to cause a reduction in unemployment.

_____ 12.   An auto manufacturer should continue to produce additional automobiles as long as the firm is profitable, even if the cost of the additional units exceeds the price received.

_____ 13.   An individual wheat farmer is likely to have market power.

_____ 14.   To a student, the opportunity cost of going to a basketball game would include the price of the ticket and the value of the time that could have been spent studying.

_____ 15.   Workers in Canada have a relatively high standard of living because Canada has a relatively high minimum wage.

_____ 16.   Room and board are opportunity costs of going to university.

B. Multiple-Choice Questions

1. Which one of the following involves a tradeoff faced by societies?
    a. buying a smart phone
    b. watching television
    c. taking a family vacation
    d. having a clean environment and a high level of income

2. Which one of the following is a reason that tradeoffs are required?
    a. Wants are unlimited and resources are efficient.
    b. Wants are unlimited and resources are economical.
    c. Wants are unlimited and resources are scarce.
    d. Wants are unlimited and resources are unlimited.

3. Which one of the following best defines what economics studies?
    a. how to avoid having to make tradeoffs
    b. how society manages its scarce resources
    c. how to fully satisfy our unlimited wants
    d. how to reduce our wants until we are satisfied

4. Which one of the following describes when a rational person will act?
    a. when the action is ethical
    b. when the action makes money for the person
    c. when the action produces marginal costs that exceed marginal benefits
    d. when the action produces marginal benefits that exceed marginal costs

5. Which one of the following is an outcome of lowering income taxes and decreasing welfare payments?
    a. reduced market power
    b. increased market power
    c. improved equity at the expense of efficiency
    d. improved efficiency at the expense of equity

6. Suppose Candace finds $20. If she chooses to use the $20 to go to a hockey game, which one of the following is her opportunity cost of going to the game?
   a. nothing, because Candace found the money
   b. $20 (because Candace could have used the $20 to buy other things)
   c. $20 (because Candace could have used the $20 to buy other things) plus the value of the time spent at the game
   d. $20 (because Candace could have used the $20 to buy other things) plus the value of the time spent at the game, plus the cost of the dinner she consumed at the game

7. Which one of the following best describes foreign trade?
   a. makes a country more equitable
   b. increases the scarcity of resources
   c. allows a country to avoid tradeoffs
   d. allows a country to have a greater variety of products at a lower cost than if it tried to produce everything at home

8. Because people respond to incentives, which one of the following would be expected to occur if the average salary of accountants increases by 50 percent, while the average salary of teachers increases by 20 percent?
   a. Fewer students will attend university.
   b. Students will shift majors from education to accounting.
   c. Students will shift majors from accounting to education.

9. Which one of the following activities is **MOST** likely to produce an externality?
   a. A student reads a novel for pleasure.
   b. A student sits at home and watches television.
   c. A student has a party in her student residence room.
   d. A student eats a hamburger in the university cafeteria.

10. Which one of the following products would be **LEAST** capable of producing an externality?
    a. hamburgers
    b. alcohol
    c. education
    d. vaccinations against disease

11. Which one of the following situations describes the **GREATEST** *market power*?
    a. Microsoft's impact on the price of desktop operating systems
    b. a farmer's impact on the price of corn
    c. Honda's impact on the price of autos
    d. a student's impact on university tuition

12. Which one of the following statements is true about a market economy?
    a. Taxes help prices communicate costs and benefits to producers and consumers.
    b. The strength of a market system is that it tends to distribute goods and services evenly across consumers.
    c. Market participants act as if guided by an "invisible hand" to produce outcomes that maximize social welfare.
    d. With a large enough computer, central planners could guide production more efficiently than markets could guide production.

13. Which one of the following is true according to Adam Smith's "invisible hand"?
    a. Markets work even in the absence of property rights.
    b. Many buyers and sellers acting independently and out of self-interest can promote general economic well-being without even realizing it.
    c. Individuals who are concerned about the public good will almost invisibly promote increased social welfare.
    d. Government plays a behind-the-scenes role in making a market economy work efficiently.

14. Which one of the following is a reason that workers in Canada enjoy a high standard of living?
    a. Canada has a high minimum wage.
    b. Unions in Canada keep wages high.
    c. Workers in Canada are highly productive.
    d. Canada has protected its industry from foreign competition.

15. Which one of the following is a cause of high and persistent inflation?
    a. unions increasing wages
    b. OPEC raising the price of oil
    c. regulations raising the cost of production
    d. governments increasing the quantity of money

16. Which of the following occurs in the short run?
    a. An increase in inflation temporarily increases unemployment.
    b. A decrease in inflation temporarily increases unemployment.
    c. Inflation and unemployment are unrelated in the short run.

17. Which one of the following could be inferred by an increase in the price of beef?
    a. It tells consumers to buy more beef.
    b. It tells consumers to buy less pork.
    c. It tells producers to produce more beef.
    d. It provides no information because prices in a market system are managed by planning boards.

18. Which one of the following is **NOT** part of the opportunity cost of going on vacation?
    a. the money spent on food
    b. the money spent on airplane tickets
    c. the money spent on a Broadway show
    d. the money that could have been earned by staying home and working

19. Which one of the following is a way that productivity can be increased?
    a. by raising union wages
    b. by raising the minimum wage
    c. by improving the education of workers
    d. by restricting trade with foreign countries

C. Short-Answer Questions

1. Is air scarce? Is clean air scarce? _____
    _____
    _____

2. What is the opportunity cost when an employee saves some of her paycheque?
    _____
    _____

3. Why is there a tradeoff between equity and efficiency? _____
    _____
    _____
    _____

4. Water is necessary for life. Diamonds are not. Is the marginal benefit of an additional glass of water greater or less than the marginal benefit of an additional one-carat diamond? Why? _____
    _____
    _____
    _____

5. Tom's car needs to be repaired. He has already paid $800 to have the transmission fixed, but it still does not work properly. Tom can sell the car "as is" for $2000. If the car was fixed, Tom could sell it for $2500. The car can be fixed, with a guarantee, for another $300. Should Tom repair his car? Why or why not?
    _____
    _____
    _____

6.   Why have automotive air bags reduced deaths from auto crashes less than we had hoped? _____

_____

_____

7.   Suppose one country is better at producing agricultural products (because it has more fertile land), while another country is better at producing manufactured goods (it has a better educational system and more engineers). If each country produced its specialty and traded, would there be more or less total output than if each country produced enough of its own agricultural and manufactured goods to meet its own needs? Why? _____

_____

_____

8.   What are the short-run effects of increasing the quantity of money?

_____

_____

_____

_____

9.   If people save more and use it to build more physical capital, productivity will rise and people will have rising standards of living in the future. What is the opportunity cost of future growth? _____

_____

_____

10. If the government printed twice as much money, what would happen to prices?

_____

_____

11. A goal for a society is to distribute resources equitably or fairly. How should resources be distributed if everyone were equally talented and worked equally hard? What if people had different talents and some people worked hard, while others did not? _____

_____

_____

12. Why are property rights important to a market economy? _____

_____

_____

D. Practice Problems

1. People respond to incentives. Governments can alter incentives with public policy, and hence behaviour. However, sometimes public policy generates unintended consequences by producing results that were not anticipated. Describe one unintended consequence of each of the following public policies.

    a. To help the "working poor," the government raises the minimum wage to $25 per hour._____

    _____

    _____

    b. To help the homeless, the government places rent controls on apartments that restrict rent to $100 per month._____

    _____

    _____

    _____

    c. To limit the consumption of gasoline, the government raises the tax on gasoline by $2.00 per litre. _____

    _____

    _____

    _____

    d. To reduce the consumption of drugs, the government makes drugs illegal.

    _____

    _____

    _____

    e. To raise the population of wolves, the government prohibits the killing of wolves._____

    _____

    _____

2. Opportunity cost is what is given up to get an item. Because there is no such thing as a free lunch, what would likely be given up to obtain each of the items listed below?

    a. Susan can work full time or go to university. She chooses university.

    _____

    _____

    b. Susan can work full time or go to university. She chooses work.

    _____

    _____

c. Farmer Jones has 100 hectares of land. He can plant corn, which yields 100 tonnes per hectare, or he can plant beans, which yield 40 tonnes per hectare. He chooses to plant corn. _____

_____

_____

d. Farmer Jones has 100 hectares of land. He can plant corn, which yields 100 tonnes per hectare, or he can plant beans, which yield 40 tonnes per hectare. He chooses to plant beans. _____

_____

_____

E. Advanced Critical Thinking

Suppose the university decides to lower the cost of parking on campus by reducing the price of a parking permit from $300 per semester to $50 per semester.

1. What would happen to the number of students desiring to park their cars on campus? _____

_____

2. What would happen to the amount of time it would take to find a parking place?

_____

_____

3. Thinking in terms of opportunity cost, would the lower price of a parking sticker necessarily lower the true cost of parking? _____

_____

_____

4. Would the opportunity cost of parking be the same for students with no outside employment and students with jobs earning $15 per hour?

_____

_____

_____

III. Solutions

A. True/False Questions

1. F; the economy becomes more equitable.
2. T
3. F; the "invisible hand" refers to how markets guide self-interested people to create desirable social outcomes.
4. T
5. F; Canada gains from trade.
6. T
7. F; higher prices reduce the quantity demanded.
8. T
9. T
10. F; high inflation is caused by excessive monetary growth.
11. F; a reduction in inflation tends to raise unemployment.
12. F; a manufacturer should produce as long as the marginal benefit exceeds the marginal cost.
13. F; a single farmer has no impact on wheat prices.
14. T
15. F; workers in Canada have a high standard of living because they are productive.
16. F; only to the extent that they are more expensive than elsewhere.

B. Multiple-Choice Questions

1. d	5. d	9. c	13. b	17. c
2. c	6. c	10. a	14. c	18. a
3. b	7. d	11. a	15. d	19. c
4. d	8. b	12. c	16. b	

C. Short-Answer Questions

1. No, no need to give up anything to get it. Yes, it is not possible to have an unlimited amount without giving up something to get it (pollution equipment on cars, etc.).

2. The items she could have enjoyed had she spent it (current consumption).

3. The goals of equity and efficiency often conflict. For example, taxes and welfare make people more equal but reduce incentives for hard work, thus lowering total output.

4. The marginal benefit of another glass of water is generally lower because the water supply is so large that one more glass is of little value. The opposite is true for diamonds.

5. Yes, because the marginal benefit of fixing the car is $2500 – $2000 = $500 and the marginal cost is $300. The original repair payment of $800 is not relevant.

6. The cost of an accident was lowered. This changed incentives, and therefore people drive faster and have more accidents.

7. There would be more total output if the countries specialize and trade because each country is doing what it does most efficiently.

8. Increasing the quantity of money stimulates the overall demand for goods and services, causing firms to increase their production of goods and services and increase their employment of workers, leading to lower unemployment. Firms may also raise their prices, leading to higher inflation.

9. The opportunity cost of future growth is the need to give up consumption today.

10. Prices would roughly double.

11. In the first case, fairness would require that everyone get an equal share. In the second case, fairness would require that people not get an equal share.

12. A farmer will not grow food if he expects his crop to be stolen. People rely on government to enforce their rights over the things they produce.

D. Practice Problems

1. a. Many would want to work at $25 per hour but few firms would want to hire low-productivity workers at this wage; therefore, it would create more unemployment.

    b. Many renters would want to rent an apartment at $100 per month, but few landlords could produce an apartment at this price; therefore, this rent control would create more homelessness.

    c. Higher gas prices would reduce the number of kilometres driven. This would lower auto accidents, put less wear and tear on roads and cars, and reduce the demand for both cars and road repairs.

    d. This raises the price of drugs and makes selling them more profitable. This creates more drug sellers and increases violence as they fight to protect their turf.

    e. Restrictions on killing wolves reduce the population of animals upon which wolves may feed, e.g., rabbits, deer.

2. a. She gives up income from work (and must pay tuition).

    b. She gives up a university degree and the increase in income throughout life that it would have brought her (but she does not have to pay tuition).

    c. He gives up 4000 tonnes of beans.

    d. He gives up 10 000 tonnes of corn.

E. Advanced Critical Thinking

1. More students would wish to park on campus.

2. It would take much longer to find a parking place.

3. No; the value of the time spent looking for a parking place would have to be factored in.

4. No. Students who could be earning money working are giving up more while looking for a parking place than those with no outside employment. Therefore, their opportunity cost is higher.

2 | Thinking Like an Economist

I. Chapter Overview

A. Context and Purpose

Chapter 2 is the second chapter in a three-chapter section that serves as the introduction of the text. Chapter 1 introduced ten principles of economics that will be revisited throughout the text. Chapter 2 develops how economists approach problems, while Chapter 3 will explain how individuals and countries gain from trade.

The purpose of Chapter 2 is to familiarize students with how economists approach economic problems. With practice, it is possible to approach similar problems in this dispassionate, systematic way. How economists employ the scientific method, the role of assumptions in model building, and the application of two specific economic models are explained. The important distinction between two roles economists can play—as scientists when they try to explain the economic world and as policymakers when they try to improve it—is clarified.

B. Helpful Hints

1. *Opportunity costs are not usually constant along a production possibilities frontier.* Notice that the production possibilities frontier shown in the following graph is bowed outward. It shows the production tradeoffs for an economy that produces only paper and pencils.

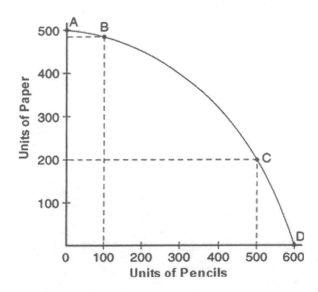

Starting at the point where the economy is using all its resources to produce paper, the production of 100 units of pencils requires a tradeoff or an opportunity cost of only 25 units of paper (point A to point B). This is because when resources are moved from paper production to pencil production, the resources that are moved first are the ones best suited for pencil production and poorly suited for paper production. Therefore, pencil production increases with very little decrease in paper production. However, if the economy were operating at point C, the opportunity cost of an additional 100 pencils (point C to D) is 200 units of paper. This is because the resources that would now be moved toward pencil production are the ones that were extremely well suited for paper production and poorly suited for pencil production. Therefore, as more and more of any particular good is produced, the opportunity cost per unit tends to rise because resources are specialized. That is, resources are not equally well suited for producing each output.

The argument above applies when moving in either direction on the production possibilities frontier. For example, by starting at point D (maximum production of pencils), a small reduction in pencil production (100 units) releases enough resources to increase production of paper by a large amount (200 units). However, moving from point B to point A increases paper production by only 25 units.

2. *A production possibilities frontier shows only the choices available—not which point of production is best.* A common mistake made by students when using production possibilities frontiers is to look at a production possibilities frontier and suggest that a point somewhere near the middle "looks best." Students make this subjective judgment because the middle point appears to provide the biggest total number of units of production of the two goods. However, ask the following question: Using the production possibilities frontier in the previous graph, what production point would be best if paper were worth $10 per sheet and pencils were worth 1 cent per dozen? The resources would be moved toward paper production. What if paper was worth 1 cent per sheet and pencils were worth $50 each? We would move our resources toward pencil production. Clearly, what we actually choose to produce depends on the price of each good. Therefore, a production possibilities frontier provides only the choices available; it alone cannot determine which choice is best.

3. *Economic disagreement is interesting but economic consensus is more important.* Economists have a reputation for disagreeing with one another because they tend to highlight their differences. While their disagreements are interesting to them, the matters on which they agree are more important to students. There are a great number of economic principles for which there is near unanimous support from the economics profession. The aim of this text is to concentrate on the areas of agreement within the profession as opposed to the areas of disagreement.

II. Self-Testing Challenges

A. True/False Questions

_____1. Economic models must mirror reality, or they are of no value.

_____2. Assumptions make the world easier to understand because they simplify reality and focus our attention.

_____3. The payments from firms to households for the use of the factors of production are wages, interest, and profit.

_____4. The factors of production that households sell to firms are labour, land, and capital.

_____5. If an economy is operating on its production possibilities frontier, it must be using its resources efficiently.

_____6. If an economy is operating on its production possibilities frontier, it must produce less of one good if it produces more of another.

_____7. Points outside the production possibilities frontier are attainable but inefficient.

_____8. If an economy were experiencing substantial unemployment, the economy is producing inside the production possibilities frontier.

_____9. The production possibilities frontier is bowed outward because the tradeoffs between the production of any two goods are constant.

_____10. An advance in production technology would cause the production possibilities curve to shift outward.

_____11. Macroeconomics is concerned with the study of how households and firms make decisions and how they interact in specific markets.

_____12. The statement, "An increase in inflation tends to cause unemployment to fall in the short run," is normative.

_____13. When economists make positive statements, they are more likely to be acting as scientists.

_____14. Microeconomics and macroeconomics both use the same set of economic models.

_____15. Most economists agree that agricultural subsidies should be enhanced.

B. Multiple-Choice Questions

1.   Which one of the following is essential to the scientific method?
     a.   that the scientist be objective
     b.   that only incorrect theories are tested
     c.   that the scientist use precision equipment
     d.   that the scientist use test tubes and have a clean lab

2.   Which one of the following is **MOST** likely to produce scientific evidence about a theory?
     a.   a radio talk-show host collecting data on how financial markets respond to taxation
     b.   a lawyer employed by General Motors addressing the impact of air bags on passenger safety
     c.   a tenured economist employed at a leading university analyzing the impact of proposed bank mergers
     d.   an economist employed by the Canadian Auto Workers union doing research on the impact of international trade

3.   Which one of the following statements regarding the circular-flow diagram is true?
     a.   The factors of production are owned by firms.
     b.   The factors of production are owned by households.
     c.   If Molson sells a case of beer, the transaction takes place in the market for factors of production.
     d.   If Susan works for Bell Canada and receives a paycheque, the transaction takes place in the market for goods and services.

4.   Which one of the following cases presents the **MOST** reasonable assumption?
     a.   To address the benefits of trade, an economist assumes that there are two people and two goods.
     b.   To estimate the speed at which a beach ball falls, a physicist assumes that it falls in a vacuum.
     c.   To address the impact of money growth on inflation, an economist assumes that money is strictly coins.
     d.   To address the impact of taxes on income distribution, an economist assumes that everyone earns the same income.

5.   Which one of the following statements is true of economic models?
     a.   built with assumptions
     b.   useless if they are simple
     c.   created to duplicate reality
     d.   usually made of wood and plastic

6. Which one of the following is **NOT** a factor of production?
   a. land
   b. labour
   c. capital
   d. money

7. Which one of the following refers to points inside the production possibilities frontier?
   a. efficient
   b. inefficient
   c. unattainable
   d. normative

8. Which one of the following will **NOT** shift a country's production possibilities frontier outward?
   a. an increase in the capital stock
   b. an advance in technology
   c. a reduction in unemployment
   d. an increase in the labour force

9. Which one of the following is a depiction of economic growth?
   a. a movement from inside the curve toward the curve
   b. a shift in the production possibilities frontier outward
   c. a shift in the production possibilities frontier inward
   d. a movement along a production possibilities frontier toward capital goods

Use the following graph to answer questions 10–13.

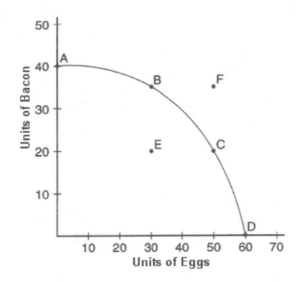

10.   If the economy is operating at point C, which one of the following is the opportunity cost of producing an additional 15 units of bacon?
a.   10 units of eggs
b.   20 units of eggs
c.   30 units of eggs
d.   40 units of eggs

11.   Which of the following is true if the economy is operating at point E?
a.   The opportunity cost of 20 additional units of eggs is 10 units of bacon.
b.   The opportunity cost of 20 additional units of eggs is 20 units of bacon.
c.   The opportunity cost of 20 additional units of eggs is 30 units of bacon.
d.   Twenty additional units of eggs can be produced with no impact on bacon production.

12.   Which one of the following is represented by point F?
a.   a combination of production that is inefficient because there are unemployed resources
b.   a combination of production that can be reached if we reduce the production of eggs by 20 units
c.   a combination of production that can be reached if there is a sufficient advance in technology
d.   a combination of production that can be reached if we reduce the production of eggs by 15 units

13.   Which one of the following statements represents the results of a move from point A to point D?
a.   The economy becomes more efficient.
b.   The opportunity cost of eggs in terms of bacon falls.
c.   The opportunity cost of eggs in terms of bacon rises.
d.   The opportunity cost of eggs in terms of bacon is constant.

14.   Which one of the following issues is related to macroeconomics?
a.   the impact of growth in the quantity of money on inflation
b.   the impact of rising gasoline prices on car sales
c.   the impact of government regulation on the airline industry
d.   the impact of foreign competition on the wine industry in Canada

15.   Which one of the following statements about microeconomics and macroeconomics is **NOT** true?
a.   Microeconomics is a building block for macroeconomics.
b.   Macroeconomics is concerned with economy-wide phenomena.
c.   Microeconomics and macroeconomics each has its own set of models.
d.   The study of very large industries is a topic within macroeconomics.

16. Which one of the following statements is normative?
    a. Printing too much money causes inflation.
    b. People work harder if the wage is higher.
    c. The unemployment rate should be lower.
    d. Large government deficits cause an economy to grow more slowly.

17. In which one of the following statements made by an economist is the economist acting more like a scientist?
    a. The rate of inflation should be reduced because it robs the elderly of their savings.
    b. A reduction in employment insurance benefits will reduce the unemployment rate.
    c. The unemployment rate should be reduced because unemployment robs individuals of their dignity.
    d. The government should increase subsidies to universities because the future of our country depends on education.

18. Which of the following most represents positive statements?
    a. microeconomic
    b. macroeconomic
    c. statements of description that can be tested
    d. statements of prescription that involve value judgments

19. Suppose two economists are arguing about policies that deal with unemployment. One economist says, "The government should fight unemployment because it is the greatest social evil." The other economist responds, "Hogwash. Inflation is the greatest social evil." Which one of the following summarizes the positions of these two economists?
    a. They disagree because they have different values.
    b. They really do not disagree at all—it just looks that way.
    c. They disagree because at least one of them is incompetent.
    d. They disagree because they have different scientific judgments.

20. Suppose two economists are arguing about policies that deal with unemployment. One economist says, "The government could lower unemployment by one percentage point if it would just increase government spending by $5 billion." The other economist responds, "Hogwash. If the government spent an additional $5 billion, it would reduce unemployment by only one-tenth of one percent, and that effect would only be temporary!" Which one of the following summarizes the positions of these two economists?
    a. They disagree because they have different values.
    b. They really do not disagree at all; it just looks that way.
    c. They disagree because at least one of them is incompetent.
    d. They disagree because they have different scientific judgments.

C. Short-Answer Questions

1.   Describe the scientific method._____

_____

_____

2.   What is the role of households in the two types of markets in the circular flow model? _____

_____

_____

3.   What is the role of firms in the two types of markets in the circular flow model?

_____

_____

4.   Why would a production possibilities frontier have a negative slope (slope down and to the right)? _____

_____

_____

5.   Why is the production possibilities frontier bowed outward?

_____

_____

6.   What are the two subfields within economics? Which is more likely to be a building block of the other? Why? _____

_____

_____

_____

7.   When an economist makes a normative statement, is he or she more likely to be acting as a scientist or a policymaker? Why? _____

_____

_____

8.   Which statements are testable: positive statements or normative statements? Why? _____

_____

_____

9.   Provide two reasons why economists disagree. _____

_____

_____

10. Name two economic propositions on which more than 90 percent of economists agree. _____

_____

_____

D. Practice Problems

1. Identify the parts of the circular-flow diagram immediately involved in the following transactions.

a. Mary buys a car from General Motors for $25 000.

_____

_____

_____

_____

b. General Motors pays Joe $5000 per month for work on the assembly line.

_____

_____

_____

_____

c. Joe gets a $15 haircut. _____

_____

_____

_____

d. Mary receives $10 000 of dividends on her General Motors stock.

_____

_____

_____

2. The following table provides information about the production possibilities frontier of Athletic Country.

Baseball bats	Tennis racquets
0	420
100	400
200	360
300	300
400	200
500	0

a. Plot and connect these points to create Athletic Country's production possibilities frontier.

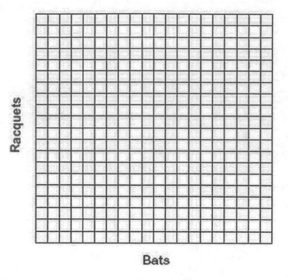

Racquets

Bats

b. If Athletic Country currently produces 100 baseball bats and 400 tennis racquets, what is the opportunity cost of an additional 100 bats?

_____

_____

c. If Athletic Country currently produces 300 baseball bats and 300 tennis racquets, what is the opportunity cost of an additional 100 bats?

_____

_____

d. Why does the additional production of 100 bats in part (c) cause a greater tradeoff than the additional production of 100 bats in part (b)?

_____

_____

_____

e. Suppose Athletic Country is currently producing 200 baseball bats and 200 tennis racquets. How many additional bats could it produce without giving up any racquets? How many additional racquets could it produce without giving up any bats? _____

_____

_____

f. Is the production of 200 bats and 200 racquets efficient? Explain.

_____

_____

3. The following production possibilities frontier shows the available tradeoffs between consumption goods and capital goods. Suppose two countries face the identical production possibilities frontier shown below.

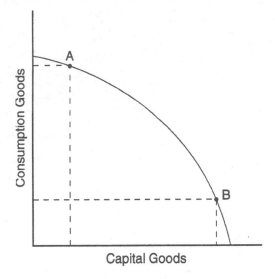

a. Suppose Party Country chooses to produce at point A, while Parsimonious Country chooses to produce at point B. Which country will experience more growth in the future? Why? _____

   _____

   _____

b. In this model, what is the opportunity cost of future growth?

   _____

c. Demonstrate the impact of economic growth on a production possibilities frontier such as the one shown above. Would the production possibilities frontier for Parsimonious Country shift more or less than that for Party Country? Why? _____

   _____

   _____

d. Suppose there was an increase in technology that affected only the production of capital goods. Show the shift in the production possibilities curve.

e. Does the shift in part (d) above imply that all additional production must be in the form of capital goods? Why or why not? _____

_____

_____

E. Advanced Critical Thinking

Kathy is watching *The National* on CBC. On the program, there is a discussion of the pros and cons of free trade (lack of obstructions to international trade). For balance, there are two economists present—one in support of free trade and one opposed. Kathy thinks to herself, "Those economists have no idea what's going on. They cannot agree on anything. One says free trade makes us rich. The other says it will drive us into poverty. If the experts do not know, how is the average person ever going to know whether free trade is best?"

1. Why might the economists be disagreeing on this issue?

    _____

    _____

2. Suppose that 93 percent of economists believe that free trade is generally best (which is the greatest agreement on any single issue). Is it now possible to give a more precise answer about why economists might disagree on this issue?

    _____

    _____

3. What if it was later discovered that the economist opposed to free trade worked for a labour union. Would that help explain why there appears to be a difference of opinion on this issue? _____

    _____

    _____

III. Solutions

A. True/False Questions

1. F; economic models are simplifications of reality.
2. T
3. F; the payments are wages, rent, and profit.
4. T
5. T
6. T
7. F; points outside the production possibilities frontier cannot yet be attained.
8. T
9. F; it is bowed outward because the tradeoffs are not constant but are increasing.
10. T
11. F; macroeconomics is the study of economy-wide phenomena.
12. F; this statement is positive.
13. T
14. F; each field has its own set of models.
15. F; most economists agree that agricultural subsidies should be eliminated.

B. Multiple-Choice Questions

1. a	5. a	9. b	13. c	17. b
2. c	6. d	10. b	14. a	18. c
3. b	7. b	11. d	15. d	19. a
4. a	8. c	12. c	16. c	20. d

C. Short-Answer Questions

1. The scientific method is the dispassionate development and testing of theory by observing, testing, and observing again.

2. Households buy and consume goods and services in the markets for goods and services. They own and sell factors of production in the markets for factors of production.

3. Firms produce and sell goods and services in the markets for goods and services. They hire and use factors of production in the markets for factors of production.

4. If an economy is operating efficiently, production choices have opportunity costs. If we want more of one thing, we must have less of another.

5. Resources are specialized and thus are not equally well suited for producing different outputs.

6.   Microeconomics and macroeconomics. Microeconomics is more of a building block of macroeconomics. When macro issues (for example, unemployment) are analyzed, the behaviour of households and firms also needs to be considered.

7.   As a policymaker: normative statements are prescriptions about what ought to be and are somewhat based on value judgments.

8.   Positive statements are statements of fact and are refutable by examining evidence.

9.   Economists may have different scientific judgments. Economists may have different values.

10.   A ceiling on rents reduces the quantity and quality of housing available. Tariffs and import quotas usually reduce general economic welfare.

D. Practice Problems

1.   a. $25 000 of spending from households to market for goods and services. Car moves from market for goods and services to households. $25 000 of revenue from market for goods and services to firms, while car moves from firms to market for goods and services.

b. $5000 of wages from firms to market for factors of production. Inputs move from market for factors of production to firms. Labour moves from households to market for factors of production, while $5000 income moves from market for factors of production to households.

c. $15 of spending from households to market for goods and services. Service moves from market for goods and services to households. Service moves from firms to market for goods and services in return for $15 revenue.

d. $10 000 of profit from firms to market for factors of production. Capital moves from market for factors of production to firms. Capital moves from households to market for factors of production in return for $10 000 income.

2. a.

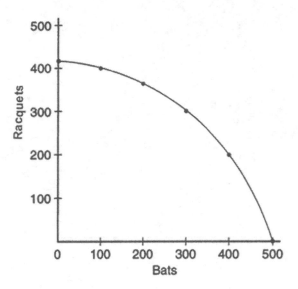

b. 40 tennis racquets

c. 100 tennis racquets

d. As more baseball bats are produced, the resources best suited for making bats are already being uscd. Therefore, it takes even more resources to produce 100 bats, causing greater reductions in racquet production.

e. 200 baseball bats; 160 tennis racquets

f. No. Resources were not used efficiently if production could be increased with no opportunity cost.

3. a. Parsimonious Country. Capital (plant and equipment) is a factor of production, and producing more of it now will increase future production.

b. Fewer consumption goods are produced now.

c.

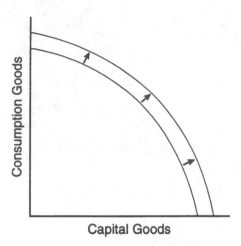

The production possibilities curve will shift more for Parsimonious Country because it has experienced a greater increase in factors of production (capital).

d.

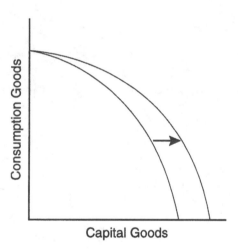

e. No. The outward shift improves choices available for both consumption and capital goods.

E. Advanced Critical Thinking

1. Economists may have different scientific judgments. Economists may have different values.

2. Those opposed to free trade are likely to have different values. There is not much disagreement on this issue within the mainstream economics profession.

3. Yes. It suggests that impediments to international trade may benefit some groups (unionized labour) but these impediments are unlikely to benefit the public in general. Those opposed to free trade are promoting their own interests.

IV. APPENDIX: Graphing: A Brief Review

A. True/False Questions

_____1.   When graphing in the coordinate system, the x-coordinate tells us the horizontal location of the point, while the y-coordinate tells us the vertical location of the point.

_____2.   When a line slopes upward in the coordinate system, the two variables measured on each axis are positively related.

_____3.   Price and quantity demanded for **MOST** goods are positively related.

_____4.   If three variables are related, one of them must be held constant when graphing the other two in the coordinate system.

_____5.   If three variables are related, a change in the variable not represented on the coordinate system will cause a movement along the curve drawn in the coordinate system.

_____6.   The slope of a line is equal to the change in y divided by the change in x along the line.

_____7.   When a line has a negative slope, the two variables measured on each axis are positively related.

_____8.   There is a positive correlation between lying down and death. If the conclusion from this evidence is that it is unsafe to lie down, then there is an omitted variable problem because critically ill people tend to lie down.

_____9.   Reverse causality means that, while people think A causes B, B may actually cause A.

_____10. Because people carry umbrellas to work in the morning and it rains later in the afternoon, carrying umbrellas must cause rain.

B. Practice Problems

1. The following ordered pairs of price and quantity demanded describe Joe's demand for cups of gourmet coffee:

Price per cup of coffee	Quantity demanded of coffee
$5	2 cups
$4	4 cups
$3	6 cups
$2	8 cups
$1	10 cups

    a. Plot and connect the ordered pairs on the graph provided below.

    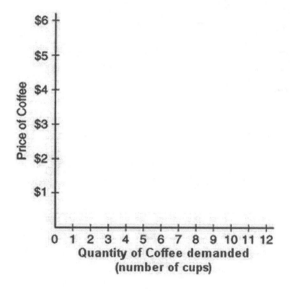

    b. What is the slope of Joe's demand curve for coffee in the price range of $5 and $4?

    _____

    _____

    c. What is the slope of Joe's demand curve for coffee in the price range of $2 and $1? _____

    _____

    _____

    d. Are the price of coffee and Joe's quantity demanded of coffee positively related or negatively related? How can you tell? _____

    _____

    _____

e. If the price of coffee moves from $2 per cup to $4 per cup, what happens to the quantity demanded? Is this a movement along a curve or a shift in the curve? _____

_____

_____

f. Suppose Joe's income doubles from $20 000 per year to $40 000 per year. Now the following ordered pairs describe Joe's demand for gourmet coffee. Plot these ordered pairs on the graph provided in part (a) above.

Price per cup of coffee	Quantity demanded of coffee
$5	4 cups
$4	6 cups
$3	8 cups
$2	10 cups
$1	12 cups

g. Did the doubling of Joe's income cause a movement along his demand curve or a shift in his demand curve? Why? _____

_____

_____

2. An alien lands on earth and observes the following: On mornings when people carry umbrellas, it tends to rain later in the day. The alien concludes that umbrellas cause rain.

a. What error has the alien committed? _____

_____

_____

b. What role did *expectations* play in the alien's error?

_____

_____

c. If rain is truly caused by humidity, temperature, wind currents, and so on, what additional type of error has the alien committed when it decided that umbrellas cause rain? _____

_____

_____

V. Solutions for Appendix

A. True/False Questions

1. T
2. T
3. F; they are negatively related.
4. T
5. F; a change in a variable not represented on the graph will cause a shift in the curve.
6. T
7. F; negative slope implies a negative relation.
8. T
9. T
10. F; this is an example of reverse causation.

B. Practice Problems

1. a.

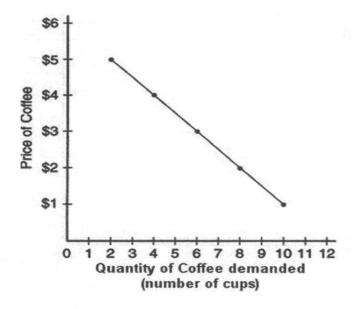

   b. −0.5

   c. −0.5

   d. Negatively related; an increase in price is associated with a decrease in quantity demanded; i.e., the demand curve slopes downward.

   e. decrease by 4 cups; movement along curve

f.

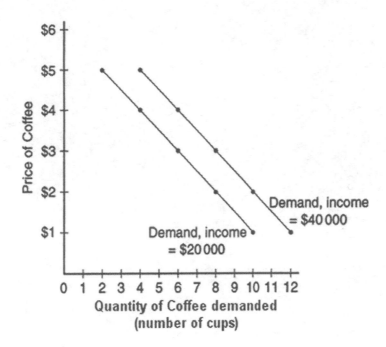

g. Shift in his demand curve because a variable changed (income) that is not measured on either axis.

2. a. reverse causality

b. Because rain can be predicted, people's expectation of rain causes them to carry umbrellas before it rains, making it appear as if umbrellas cause rain.

c. omitted variables

3 Interdependence and the Gains from Trade

I. Chapter Overview

A. Context and Purpose

Chapter 3 is the third chapter in the three-chapter section that serves as the introduction of the text. The first chapter introduced ten fundamental principles of economics. The second chapter developed how economists approach problems. This chapter shows how people and countries gain from trade (which is one of the ten principles discussed in Chapter 1).

The purpose of Chapter 3 is to demonstrate how everyone can gain from trade. Trade allows people to specialize in the production of things for which they have a comparative advantage and then exchange them for things that other people produce. Because of specialization, total output rises and through trade people are all able to share in the bounty. This is as true for countries as it is for individuals. Since everyone can gain from trade, restrictions on trade tend to reduce welfare.

B. Helpful Hints

1. *A step-by-step example of comparative advantage.* What follows is an example that will demonstrate most of the concepts discussed in Chapter 3. It will provide a pattern to follow when answering questions at the end of the chapter in the text and for the problems that follow in this Study Guide.

    Suppose the following information about the productivity of industry in Japan and Korea is true.

	Output	
	Steel (units/h)	Televisions (units/h)
Japan	6	3
Korea	8	2

A Japanese worker can produce 6 units of steel or 3 units of televisions per hour. A Korean worker can produce 8 units of steel or 2 units of televisions per hour.

The production possibilities frontier for each country can be plotted, assuming each country has only one worker and the worker works only one hour. To plot the frontier, plot the end points and connect them with a line. For example, Japan can produce 6 units of steel with its worker or 3 units of televisions. It can also allocate one half hour to the production of each and get 3 units of steel and 1.5 televisions.

Any other proportion of the hour can be allocated to the two productive activities. The production possibilities frontier is linear in these cases because the labour resource can be moved from the production of one good to the other at a constant rate. The same can be done for Korea. Without trade, the production possibilities frontier is the consumption possibilities frontier, too.

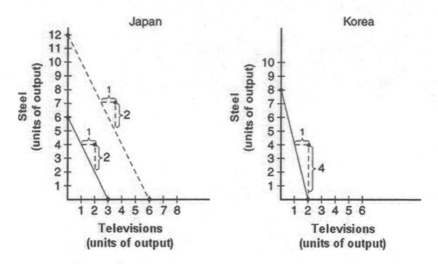

Comparative advantage determines specialization and trade. The opportunity cost of a television in Japan is 2 units of steel, which is shown by the slope of the production possibilities frontier in the previous graph. Alternatively, the opportunity cost of 1 unit of steel in Japan is one-half of a television. In Korea, the opportunity cost of a television is 4 units of steel and the cost of 1 unit of steel is one-quarter of a television. Because the opportunity cost of a television is lower in Japan, Japan has a comparative advantage in television production and should specialize in televisions. Because the opportunity cost of steel is lower in Korea, Korea has a comparative advantage in steel production and should specialize in steel.

What is the range of prices at which each country would be willing to exchange? If Japan specializes in television production and produces 3 televisions, it would be willing to trade televisions for steel as long as the price of steel is below one-half a television per unit of steel because that was the Japanese price for 1 unit of steel prior to trade. Korea would be willing to specialize in steel production and trade for televisions as long as the price of a television is less than 4 units of steel because that was the Korean price of a television prior to trade. In short, the final price must be between the original tradeoffs each faced in the absence of trade. One television will cost between 2 and 4 of units of steel. One unit of steel will cost between one-half and one-quarter of a television.

2. *Trade allows countries to consume outside their original production possibilities frontier.* Suppose that Japan and Korea settle on a trading price of 3 units of steel for 1 television (or one-third of a television for 1 unit of steel). (This price is provided. There is nothing in the problem that would permit the final trading price to be calculated. It is possible to calculate only the range in which it must lie.)

This price is halfway between the two prices that each faces in the absence of trade. The range for the trading price is 4 units of steel for 1 television to 2 units of steel for 1 television.

If Japan specializes in television production, produces 3 televisions, and exports 1 television for 3 units of steel, Japan will be able to consume 2 televisions and 3 units of steel. When this point (2 televisions and 3 units of steel) is plotted on Japan's graph, it lies outside its production possibilities frontier. If Korea specializes, produces 8 units of steel, and exports 3 units for 1 television, Korea will be able to consume 5 units of steel and 1 television. When this point (5 units of steel and 1 television) is plotted on Korea's graph, it also lies outside its production possibilities frontier.

This is the gain from trade. Trade allows countries (and people) to specialize. Specialization increases world output. After trading, countries consume outside their individual production possibilities frontiers. In this way, trade is like an improvement in technology. It allows countries to move beyond their current production possibilities frontiers.

3. *Only comparative advantage matters; absolute advantage is irrelevant.* In the previous example, Japan had an absolute advantage in the production of televisions because it could produce 3 per hour, while Korea could produce only 2. Korea had an absolute advantage in the production of steel because it could produce 8 units per hour compared to 6 for Japan.

To demonstrate that comparative advantage, not absolute advantage, determines specialization and trade, the previous example is altered such that Japan has an absolute advantage in the production of both goods. To this end, suppose Japan becomes twice as productive as in the previous table. That is, a worker can now produce 12 units of steel or 6 televisions per hour.

	Output	
	Steel (units/h)	Televisions (units/h)
Japan	12	6
Korea	8	2

Now Japan has an absolute advantage in the production of both goods. Japan's new production possibilities frontier is the dashed line in the previous graph. Will this change the analysis? Not at all. The opportunity cost of each good within Japan is the same: 2 units of steel per television, or one-half of a television per unit of steel (and Korea is unaffected). For this reason, Japan still has the identical comparative advantage as before and it will specialize in television production, while Korea will specialize in steel. However, because productivity has doubled in Japan, its entire set of choices has improved, and thus its material welfare has improved.

II. Self-Testing Challenges

A. True/False Questions

_____1.   If Japan has an absolute advantage in the production of an item, it must also have a comparative advantage in the production of that item.

_____2.   Comparative advantage, not absolute advantage, determines the decision to specialize in production.

_____3.   Absolute advantage is a comparison based on productivity.

_____4.   Self-sufficiency is the best way to increase one's material welfare.

_____5.   Comparative advantage is a comparison based on opportunity cost.

_____6.   If a producer is self-sufficient, the production possibilities frontier is also the consumption possibilities frontier.

_____7.   If a country's workers can produce 6 pencils per hour or 18 rulers per hour, absent trade, the price of 1 ruler is 3 pencils.

_____8.   If producers have different opportunity costs of production, trade will allow them to consume outside their production possibilities frontiers.

_____9.   Countries import goods for which they have a comparative advantage.

_____10.   Hard work can enhance comparative advantage.

_____11.   The gains from trade can be measured by the increase in total production and consumption that comes from specialization.

_____12.   When a country removes a specific import restriction, it always benefits every worker in that country.

_____13.   Canada has a comparative advantage in the production of pulp and paper.

_____14.   If an advanced country has an absolute advantage in the production of everything, it will benefit if it eliminates trade with less developed countries and becomes completely self-sufficient.

_____15.   If gains from trade are based solely on comparative advantage, and if all countries have the same opportunity costs of production, then there are no gains from trade.

B. Multiple Choice Questions

1. Which one of the following situations is most likely for a nation that has an **absolute** advantage in the production of a good?
   a. It can benefit by restricting imports of that good.
   b. It will specialize in the production of that good and export it.
   c. It can produce that good using fewer resources than its trading partner.
   d. It can produce that good at a lower opportunity cost than its trading partner.

2. Which one of the following situations is most likely for a nation that has a **comparative** advantage in the production of a good?
   a. It can benefit by restricting imports of that good.
   b. It must be the only country with the ability to produce that good.
   c. It can produce that good at a lower opportunity cost than its trading partner.
   d. It can produce that good using fewer resources than its trading partner.

3. Which one of the following statements about trade is true?
   a. People who are skilled at all activities cannot benefit from trade.
   b. Unrestricted international trade benefits every person in a country equally.
   c. Trade can benefit everyone in society because it allows people to specialize in activities in which they have an absolute advantage.
   d. Trade can benefit everyone in society because it allows people to specialize in activities in which they have a comparative advantage.

4. Which one of the following does the principle of comparative advantage state?
   a. Countries with a comparative advantage in the production of every good need not specialize.
   b. Countries should specialize in the production of goods that they enjoy consuming more than other countries enjoy consuming them.
   c. Countries should specialize in the production of goods for which they use fewer resources in production than do their trading partners.
   d. Countries should specialize in the production of goods for which they have a lower opportunity cost of production than do their trading partners.

5. Which one of the following statements is true?
   a. Innate talent is the sole reason that individuals rise to the top of their professions.
   b. The United States has a comparative advantage in the production of pulp and paper.
   c. Canada has a comparative advantage in the production of natural resources.
   d. Education does not create comparative advantage.

6.   Suppose a country's workers can produce 6 hats per hour or 24 ties per hour. Which one of the following is the domestic price of 1 tie if there is no trade?
a.   The domestic price of 1 tie is one-quarter of a hat.
b.   The domestic price of 1 tie is one-third of a hat.
c.   The domestic price of 1 tie is 3 hats.
d.   The domestic price of 1 tie is 4 hats.

7.   Suppose a country's workers can produce 6 hats per hour or 24 ties per hour. Which one of the following is the opportunity cost of 1 hat if there is no trade?
a.   The opportunity cost of 1 hat is one-quarter of a tie.
b.   The opportunity cost of 1 hat is one-third of a tie.
c.   The opportunity cost of 1 hat is 3 ties.
d.   The opportunity cost of 1 hat is 4 ties.

The following table shows production data for Australia and Korea. Use this table for questions 8–15.

	Output	
	Food (no. units/worker/month)	Electronics (no. units/worker/month)
Australia	20	5
Korea	8	4

8.   From the production data, which one of the following statements can be made about absolute advantage?
a.   Korea has an absolute advantage in the production of both food and electronics.
b.   Australia has an absolute advantage in the production of both food and electronics.
c.   Australia has an absolute advantage in the production of food, while Korea has an absolute advantage in the production of electronics.
d.   Korea has an absolute advantage in the production of food, while Australia has an absolute advantage in the production of electronics.

9.   Which one of the following is the opportunity cost of 1 unit of electronics in Australia?
a.   5 units of food
b.   one-fifth of a unit of food
c.   4 units of food
d.   one-quarter of a unit of food

10.   Which one of the following is the opportunity cost of 1 unit of electronics in Korea?
a. 2 units of food
b. one-half of a unit of food
c. 4 units of food
d. one-quarter of a unit of food

11.   Which one of the following is the opportunity cost of 1 unit of food in Australia?
a. 5 units of electronics
b. one-fifth of a unit of electronics
c. 4 units of electronics
d. one-quarter of a unit of electronics

12.   Which one of the following is the opportunity cost of 1 unit of food in Korea?
a. 2 units of electronics
b. one-half of a unit of electronics
c. 4 units of electronics
d. one-quarter of a unit of electronics

13.   Which one of the following statements can be made about comparative advantage?
a. Australia has a comparative advantage in the production of food, while Korea has a comparative advantage in the production of electronics.
b. Korea has a comparative advantage in the production of food, while Australia has a comparative advantage in the production of electronics.
c. Australia has a comparative advantage in the production of both food and electronics.
d. Korea has a comparative advantage in the production of both food and electronics.

14.   Which recommendation below would be the best for Korea?
a. specialize in food production, export food, and import electronics
b. specialize in electronics production, export electronics, and import food
c. produce both goods because neither country has a comparative advantage
d. produce neither good because it has an absolute disadvantage in the production of both goods

15.   Prices of electronics can be stated in terms of units of food. Which one of the following is the range of prices of electronics for which both countries could gain from trade?
a. The price must be greater than 4 units of food but less than 5 units of food.
b. The price must be greater than 2 units of food but less than 4 units of food.
c. The price must be greater than one-quarter of a unit of food but less than one-half of a unit of food.
d. The price must be greater than one-fifth of a unit of food but less than one-quarter of a unit of food.

16.   Suppose the world consists of two countries: the United States and Canada. Further, suppose there are only two goods: food and clothing. Which one of the following statements best represents the situation?
   a. If the United States has an absolute advantage in the production of food, then Canada must have an absolute advantage in the production of clothing.
   b. If the United States has a comparative advantage in the production of food, Canada might also have a comparative advantage in the production of food.
   c. If the United States has a comparative advantage in the production of food, it must also have a comparative advantage in the production of clothing.
   d. If the United States has a comparative advantage in the production of food, then Canada must have a comparative advantage in the production of clothing.

Use the following production possibilities frontiers to answer questions 17–19. Assume each country has 20 workers and that each axis is measured in tonnes per month.

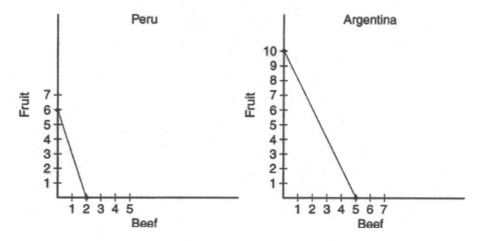

17.   For which one of the following does Argentina have a comparative advantage in production?
   a. fruit
   b. beef
   c. both fruit and beef
   d. neither fruit nor beef

18.   Which one of the following will Peru export?
   a. beef
   b. fruit
   c. both fruit and beef
   d. neither fruit nor beef

19.   Which one of the following is the opportunity cost of producing a tonne of beef in Peru?
   a. one-third of a tonne of fruit
   b. 1 tonne of fruit
   c. 2 tonnes of fruit
   d. 3 tonnes of fruit

20. Jane is a tax accountant. She receives $200 per hour for preparing tax returns. She can type 4000 characters per hour into spreadsheets. She can hire an assistant who types 1000 characters per hour into spreadsheets. Which one of the following statements is the best recommendation?
    a. Jane should not hire an assistant because the assistant cannot type as fast as she can.
    b. Jane should hire the assistant as long as she pays the assistant less than $200 per hour.
    c. Jane should hire the assistant as long as she pays the assistant less than $100 per hour.
    d. Jane should hire the assistant as long as she pays the assistant less than $50 per hour.

C. Short-Answer Questions

1. Why do people choose to become interdependent as opposed to self-sufficient?
   _____
   _____

2. Why is comparative advantage instead of absolute advantage important in determining trade? _____
   _____
   _____
   _____

3. What are the gains from trade? _____
   _____
   _____
   _____

4. Why is a restriction of trade likely to reduce economic welfare?
   _____
   _____

5. Suppose that a lawyer earning $200 per hour can also type at 200 words per minute. Should the lawyer hire a secretary who can type only 50 words per minute? Why or why not? _____
   _____

6. Evaluate this statement: A technologically advanced country, which is better than its neighbour at producing everything, would be better off if it closed its borders to trade because the less productive country is a burden to the advanced country.
   _____
   _____
   _____
   _____

D. Practice Problems

1. Angela is a college student. She takes a full load of classes and has only 5 hours per week for her hobby. Angela is artistic and can make 2 clay pots per hour or 4 coffee mugs per hour.

   a. Draw Angela's production possibilities frontier for pots and mugs based on the amount produced per week.

   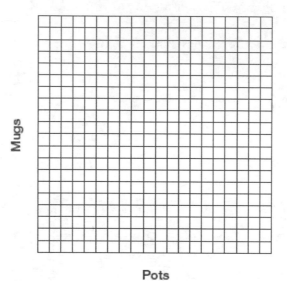

   Mugs

   Pots

   b. What is Angela's opportunity cost of 1 pot? 10 pots? _____
   _____
   _____

   c. What is Angela's opportunity cost of 1 mug? 10 mugs? _____
   _____
   _____

   d. Why is her production possibilities frontier a straight line instead of bowed out like those presented in Chapter 2? _____
   _____
   _____

2. Suppose a worker in Germany can produce 15 computers or 5 tonnes of grain per month. Suppose a worker in Poland can produce 4 computers or 4 tonnes of grain per month. For simplicity, assume that each country has only one worker.

a. Fill out the following table:

Output

	Computers (no./worker/month)	Grain (tonnes/worker/month)
Germany		
Poland		

b. Graph the production possibilities frontier for each country.

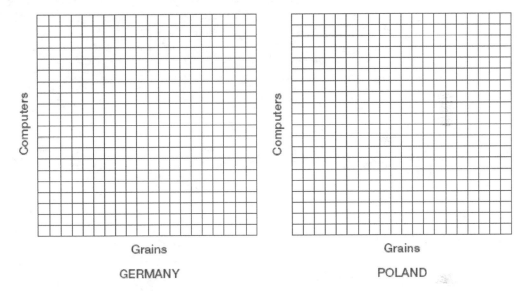

GERMANY   POLAND

c. What is the opportunity cost of 1 computer in Germany? What is the opportunity cost of 1 tonne of grain in Germany? _____

_____

d. What is the opportunity cost of 1 computer in Poland? What is the opportunity cost of 1 tonne of grain in Poland? _____

_____

e. Which country has the absolute advantage in producing computers? Grain? Why? _____

_____

f. Which country has the comparative advantage in producing computers? Grain? Why? _____

_____

_____

_____

g. Each country should tend toward specialization in the production of which good? Why? _____

_____

_____

_____

h. What are the range of prices for computers and grain for which both countries would benefit? _____

_____

_____

i. Suppose Germany and Poland settle on a price of 2 computers for 1 tonne of grain or 0.5 tonnes of grain for a computer. Suppose each country specializes completely in production and they trade 4 computers for 2 tonnes of grain. Plot the final consumption points on the graphs made in part (b) above. Are these countries consuming inside or outside their production possibilities frontier. _____

_____

_____

j. Suppose the productivity of a worker in Poland doubles so that a worker can produce 8 computers or 8 tonnes of grain per month. Which country has the absolute advantage in producing computers? Grain? _____

_____

_____

k. After the doubling of productivity in Poland, which country has a comparative advantage in producing computers? Grain? Has the comparative advantage changed? Has the economic welfare of either country changed?

_____

_____

_____

l. How would the analysis change if it was assumed, more realistically, that each country had 10 million workers? _____

_____

_____

3. Suppose a worker in Canada can produce 4 cars or 20 computers per month, while a worker in Russia can produce 1 car or 5 computers per month. Again, for simplicity, assume each country has only one worker.

a. Fill out the following table:

Output

	Cars (no./worker/month)	Computers (no./worker/month)
Canada		
Russia		

b. Which country has the absolute advantage in the production of cars? Computers? Why? _____
_____
_____

c. Which country has the comparative advantage in the production of cars? Computers? Why? _____
_____
_____
_____

d. Are there any gains to be made from trade? Why or why not? _____
_____
_____

e. Does the answer in (d) above help pinpoint a source for gains from trade?
_____
_____

f. What might make two countries have different opportunity costs of production? _____
_____
_____

E. Advanced Critical Thinking

In an election debate a candidate says, "We need to stop the flow of foreign automobiles into our country. If we limit the importation of automobiles, our domestic auto production will rise and Canada will be better off."

1. Is it likely that Canada will be better off if it limits auto imports? Explain.

    _____

    _____

2. Will anyone in Canada be better off if it limits auto imports? Explain.

    _____

    _____

3. In the real world, does every person in the country gain when restrictions on imports are reduced? Explain. _____

    _____

    _____

III. Solutions

A. True/False Questions

1. F; absolute advantage compares the quantities of inputs used in production, while comparative advantage compares the opportunity costs.
2. T
3. T
4. F; restricting trade eliminates gains from trade.
5. T
6. T
7. F; the price of 1 ruler is one-third of a pencil.
8. T
9. F; countries export goods in which they have a comparative advantage.
10. T
11. T
12. F; it may harm those involved in that industry.
13. T
14. F; voluntary trade benefits all traders.
15. T

B. Multiple-Choice Questions

1. c	5. c	9. c	13. a	17. b
2. c	6. a	10. a	14. b	18. b
3. d	7. d	11. d	15. b	19. d
4. d	8. b	12. b	16. d	20. d

C. Short-Answer Questions

1. A consumer gets a greater variety of goods at a much lower cost than he or she could produce by himself or herself. That is, there are gains from trade.

2. What is important in trade is how a country's costs without trade differ from another country's costs. This is determined by the relative opportunity costs across countries.

3. The gains from trade are additional output and consumption that comes from countries with different opportunity costs of production specializing in the production of the item for which they have the lower domestic opportunity cost.

4. It forces people to produce at a higher cost than they would pay when they trade.

5. Yes, as long as the secretary earns less than $50 per hour, the lawyer is ahead.

6. This is not true. All countries can gain from trade if their opportunity costs of production differ. Even the least productive country will have a comparative advantage at producing something, and it can trade this good to the advanced country for less than the advanced country's opportunity cost.

D. Practice Problems

1. a.

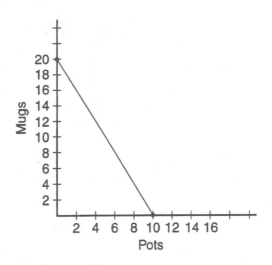

    b. 2 mugs; 20 mugs

    c. one-half of a pot; 5 pots

    d. Her resources can be moved from the production of one good to another at a constant rate.

2. a.

	Output	
	Computers (no./worker/month)	Grain (no./worker/month)
Germany	15	5
Poland	4	4

b.

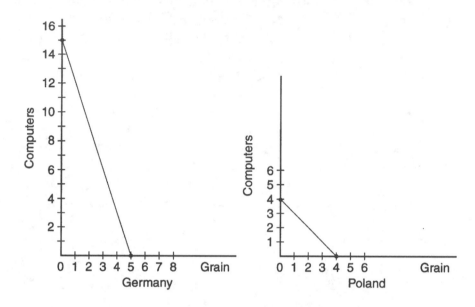

c. one-third of a tonne of grain; 3 computers

d. 1 tonne of grain; 1 computer

e. Germany, because 1 worker can produce 15 compared to 4. Germany, because 1 worker can produce 5 compared to 4.

f. Germany, because a computer has the opportunity cost of only one-third of a tonne of grain compared to 1 tonne of grain in Poland. Poland, because 1 tonne of grain has the opportunity cost of only 1 computer, compared to 3 computers in Germany.

g. Germany should produce computers, while Poland should produce grain because the opportunity cost of computers is lower in Germany and the opportunity cost of grain is lower in Poland. That is, each has a comparative advantage in those goods.

h. Grain must cost more than 1 computer and less than 3 computers. Computers must cost more than one-third of a tonne of grain and less than 1 tonne of grain.

i.

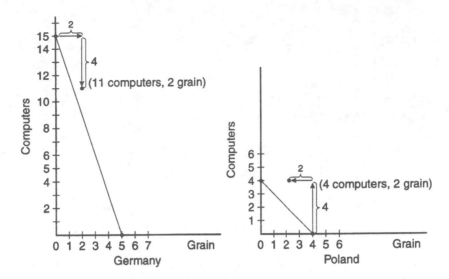

They are consuming outside their production possibilities frontier.

j.   Germany, because 1 worker can produce 15 compared to 8. Poland, because 1 worker can produce 8 compared to 5.

k.   Germany has a comparative advantage in computers. Poland has a comparative advantage in grain. No change in comparative advantage. Poland is better off, however, because it now has a larger set of choices.

l.   It would not change absolute advantage or comparative advantage. It would change the scale in the previous two graphs by a factor of 10 million.

3.   a.

	Output	
	Cars (no./worker/month)	Computers (no./worker/month)
Canada	4	20
Russia	1	5

b.   Canada, because 1 worker can produce 4 compared to 1. Canada, because 1 worker can produce 20 compared to 5.

c.   In both, the opportunity cost of 1 car is 5 computers. In both, the opportunity cost of 1 computer is one-fifth of a car. Therefore, neither has a comparative advantage in either good.

d.   No. Each can get the same tradeoff between goods domestically.

    e. Yes. There needs to be differences in opportunity costs of producing goods across countries for there to be gains from trade.

    f. Resources or technology might be different across countries. That is, workers could be differently educated, land could be of different quality, or the available technology might be different.

E. Advanced Critical Thinking

1. No. If Canada imports autos, it is because the opportunity cost of producing them elsewhere is lower than in Canada.

2. Yes. Those associated with the domestic auto industry: shareholders (owners) of domestic auto producers and autoworkers.

3. No. When we reduce restrictions on imports, the country gains from the increased trade but individuals in the affected domestic industry may lose.

4 The Market Forces of Supply and Demand

I. Chapter Overview

A. Context and Purpose

Earlier chapters provided an overview of the "economic way of thinking" in order to explain the operation of a market economy such as that of Canada. One of the cornerstones of a market economy is the interaction of supply and demand. Unfortunately, these terms are not well understood—a parrot can be taught to squawk "supply and demand" without any knowledge of the concepts. In reading the newspapers on any given day, examples of the misuse of supply and demand can be found. The terms take on a very specific meaning in economics that differs from their everyday use. This chapter explains what an economist means by supply and demand and shows how they interact to determine prices and quantities of goods and services. It also shows how various factors that change either supply or demand ultimately lead to changes in market prices and quantities.

B. Helpful Hints

1. *Supply means willingness to sell.* In everyday usage, supply often refers to physical stocks of a product or resource in the form of inventories available for sale. In economics, however, **supply** means ***willingness to sell***. For example, the newspapers often report changes in global petroleum supplies, when really they mean inventories or petroleum reserves. The supply of petroleum is the willingness to sell those reserves, not the stock of petroleum itself.

2. *Demand means willingness to buy.* Demand is not simply consumer wants. Demand represents wants backed up by dollars and willingness to spend them.

3. *A market is a collection of buyers and sellers.* Markets are not physical locations; rather, they are the interaction of buyers and sellers. Such interaction *can* occur at a physical location: for example, an auction may represent a separate market. However, buyers and sellers can interact on a national or even global level, particularly as electronic communications grow. Money markets, for example, involve buyers and sellers around the world.

4. *"Demand" is the entire schedule or curve.* Demand refers to the whole demand schedule or demand curve, not just a point on the curve. It represents all the price–quantity combinations that are acceptable to consumers. Because of this, increased sales that occur due to a price cut are not referred to as an increase in *demand*. There is, of course, an increase in the *quantity demanded*, but this is not an increase (or shift to the right) in demand itself.

5. *"Quantity demanded" is a point on the demand curve.* When there is a change in price, quantity demanded changes, but demand itself does not change.

6. *"Supply" is the entire schedule or curve.* Supply refers to the whole supply schedule or supply curve, not just a point on the curve. For supply to shift, the underlying factors that are held constant in plotting a supply curve must change. Changing the price simply means that we move to a new point on the existing supply curve, which represents a new quantity. Of course an increase in price encourages suppliers to sell more; however, this response to higher price is called an increase in *quantity supplied*, rather than an increase (or shift) in *supply*.

7. *"Quantity supplied" is a point on the supply curve.* When there is a change in price, the quantity supplied changes, even though the supply curve itself does not shift. The quantity supplied at a particular price is the amount that sellers are willing to sell at that price.

II. Self-Testing Challenges

A. True/False Questions

_____1. A decrease in the price of soft drinks will increase their demand (shift the curve to the right).

_____2. A monopolistic market has only one seller.

_____3. At the equilibrium price, the amount that sellers are willing to sell is just equal to the amount that buyers are willing to buy.

_____4. An improvement in technology tends to reduce the supply (shift it to the left).

_____5. An increase in raw materials prices tends to reduce the supply (shift it to the left).

_____6. If sellers expect prices to rise in the future, this could cause prices to rise today by encouraging sellers to reduce their current supply in anticipation of a price hike.

_____7. A perfectly competitive market consists of products that are all slightly different from one another.

_____8. A price that is below equilibrium results in excess supply.

_____9. Excess demand tends to drive price up until the market reaches equilibrium price and quantity.

_____10. An increase in supply tends to increase equilibrium price and quantity.

_____11.   An equal increase in both supply and demand tends to increase equilibrium price and quantity.

_____12.   An increase in supply accompanied by an equal decrease in demand tends to decrease equilibrium price, while leaving equilibrium quantity unchanged.

_____13.   The market demand curve is the horizontal summation of all the individual demand curves.

_____14.   If golf clubs and golf balls are complements, then an increase in the price of golf clubs will decrease the demand for golf balls.

_____15.   If pizza and hamburgers are substitutes for each other, a decrease in the price of pizza would increase the demand for hamburgers.

B. Multiple-Choice Questions

1.   Which one of the following would decrease the demand (shift the curve to the left) for beer?
   a.   The price of a substitute, wine, falls.
   b.   The price of beer increases to $5.00 per bottle.
   c.   Bars begin giving away spicy snacks to their customers.
   d.   A new Health Canada study concludes that beer helps to reduce heart disease.

2.   If buyers believe that the price of gasoline will rise soon, which one of the following is the **MOST** likely immediate result?
   a.   an increase in the quantity demanded, due to the change in supply
   b.   a decrease (shift to the left) in the demand for gasoline, due to a shift to substitutes
   c.   a decrease (shift to the left) in the demand for gasoline, due to a change in tastes
   d.   an increase (shift to the right) in the demand for gasoline, due to a change in expectations

3.   A new technological breakthrough in genetic engineering makes it possible to grow twice as much corn per hectare as had been possible in the past. Which one of the following is the **MOST** likely outcome of this development?
   a.   an increase in the demand for corn, due to the greatly reduced price
   b.   an increase in quantity supplied, due to the increased willingness to sell corn
   c.   an increase (shift to the right) in the supply of corn, due to the reduced cost of production
   d.   a decrease (shift to the left) in the supply of corn, due to the increased costs associated with the new technology

4. A university student made the following statement to a friend at a university sporting event: "This football stadium is a good example of how unrealistic economics is: My economics professor claims that, according to a so-called 'Law of Supply,' the quantity supplied varies directly with price, yet anybody can look around and see that the quantity supplied is fixed at 10 000 seats, no matter what the price is!" Which one of the following explains what is wrong with the student's statement?

    a. Quantity supplied is not fixed at 10 000 seats; it is quantity demanded that is fixed.
    b. This is simply an exception to the Law of Supply; it does not mean that it is not relevant for most cases.
    c. Quantity supplied is not the same thing as the physical stock of a good or service that is available; rather, quantity supplied is the amount of a good that sellers are willing and able to sell.
    d. The Law of Demand is more important than the Law of Supply in these types of cases.

Use the following graph to answer questions 5–8:

The Market for Personal-Sized Pizzas

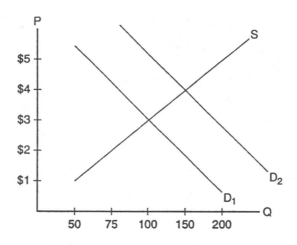

5. Referring to the graph above, which one of the following describes the initial equilibrium price and quantity?

    a. $P = \$2.00; Q = 75$
    b. $P = \$2.00; Q = 150$
    c. $P = \$3.00; Q = 100$
    d. $P = \$4.00; Q = 75$

6. Which one of the following would cause the demand for pizzas among university students to shift to the right?

    a. an increase in financial aid to university students
    b. half-price pizzas for anybody with a university ID
    c. an increase in the price of a complement, that is, beer
    d. a decrease in the price of a substitute, that is, hamburgers

7. After an increase in demand, which one of the following describes the new
    equilibrium price and quantity?
    a. $P = \$2.00$; $Q = 75$
    b. $P = \$2.00$; $Q = 150$
    c. $P = \$3.00$; $Q = 100$
    d. $P = \$4.00$; $Q = 150$

8. Which one of the following describes the effect of the increase in demand on
    supply?
    a. It would first increase, then decrease over time.
    b. It would neither rise nor fall, although quantity supplied would increase.
    c. It would decrease (shift to the left).
    d. It would increase (shift to the right).

    Use the following graph to answer questions 9–12:

    The Market for Hand-Held Calculators

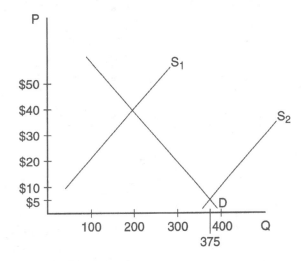

9. Referring to the graph above, which one of the following describes the initial
    equilibrium price and quantity?
    a. $P = \$5$; $Q = 375$
    b. $P = \$10$; $Q = 350$
    c. $P = \$20$; $Q = 100$
    d. $P = \$40$; $Q = 200$

10. Which one of the following is a factor that would cause an increase (shift to the
    right) in supply?
    a. improved technology
    b. higher labour costs
    c. lower number of sellers
    d. increased demand

11. Which choice below would be the new equilibrium price and quantity as a result of the increase in supply?
  e. $P = \$5; Q = 375$
  f. $P = \$10; Q = 350$
  g. $P = \$20; Q = 100$
  h. $P = \$30; Q = 250$

12. Suppose that the demand for calculators rose even more than the supply had increased. Which one of the following describes the changes in equilibrium price and quantity that would be the net effect of the two increases?
  i. an increase in price but a decrease in quantity
  j. an increase in quantity but a slight decrease in price
  k. decreases in both quantity and price
  l. increases in both quantity and price

13. Which one of the following describes what supply curves represent?
  a. inventories
  b. physical stocks
  c. total production
  d. willingness to sell

14. Which one of the following does a supply curve for a good or service show?
  a. the seller's target price
  b. the seller's minimum acceptable price
  c. the seller's maximum acceptable price
  d. the seller's average acceptable price

15. If equilibrium quantity rises but equilibrium price remains unchanged, which one of the following is the cause?
  a. an increase in both supply and demand
  b. a decrease in both demand and supply
  c. a decrease in demand and an increase in supply
  d. an increase in demand and a decrease in supply

16. If equilibrium price rises but equilibrium quantity remains unchanged, which one of the following is the cause?
  a. a decrease in demand and an increase in supply
  b. an increase in demand and a decrease in supply
  c. an increase in both supply and demand
  d. a decrease in both demand and supply

17. Suppose there is an increase in both the supply and demand for laptop computers. Which one of the following would we expect in the market for laptop computers?
   a. an increase in both equilibrium quantity and equilibrium price
   b. an increase in equilibrium quantity and a decrease in equilibrium price
   c. an increase in equilibrium quantity but the impact on equilibrium price is ambiguous
   d. a decrease in equilibrium price but the impact on equilibrium quantity is ambiguous

18. A freeze that destroys half the coffee crop in South America would likely raise the price of coffee. Which one of the following would happen in turn?
   a. reduced demand for both coffee and tea
   b. reduced quantity demanded for both coffee and tea
   c. reduced demand for coffee and increased demand for tea
   d. reduced quantity demanded for coffee and increased demand for tea

19. Which one of the following describes an inferior good?
   a. one for which demand rises as income rises
   b. one for which demand falls as income rises
   c. one for which demand is unrelated to income
   d. one for which demand is low because of the low quality of the good

20. Suppose that there is a shortage of parking spaces in downtown Toronto during weekdays. Which one of the following explains how the shortage can be eliminated?
   a. by lowering the price
   b. by decreasing the supply
   c. by allowing the price to rise
   d. by increasing the quantity demanded

C. Short-Answer Questions

1. What would happen to the demand for apples if consumers' incomes rose, and apples are a normal good? What if apples are an inferior good?

   _____

   _____

2. Explain why the price of a complement or a substitute can alter the demand for a good, even though the price of the good itself does not shift the demand.

   _____

   _____

   _____

   _____

   _____

   _____

3. What are the two main characteristics of a perfectly competitive market?

    _____

    _____

4. What are the variables that should affect the amount of a good that consumers
    wish to buy, other than its price? _____

    _____

    _____

5. What are the variables that should affect the amount of a good that producers wish
    to sell, other than its price? _____

    _____

    _____

D. Practice Problems

The supply and demand schedules below show hypothetical prices and quantities in
the market for corn. The initial quantity supplied is shown by Q^S, and the quantity
demanded is Q^D.

The Market for Corn
(in thousands of tonnes)

Price (per tonne)	Q^D	Q^S	$Q^{S'}$
$6.00	220	400	
$5.50	240	360	____
$5.00	260	320	____
$4.50	280	280	____
$4.00	300	240	____
$3.50	320	200	____
$3.00	340	160	____

1. Plot the supply and demand curves for the initial supply and demand, Q^S and Q^D,
    on the graph that follows the questions.

    a. The equilibrium price of corn is $_____ per tonne.

    b. The equilibrium quantity of corn is _____ thousand tonnes.

    c. At a price of $3.00 per tonne, there would be a (shortage, surplus) _____
        of _____ thousand tonnes, and the price would tend to (fall, rise)
        _____.

    d. At a price of $5.00 per tonne, there would be a (shortage, surplus) _____
        of _____ thousand tonnes, and the price would tend to (fall, rise)
        _____.

2. Suppose that the supply of corn increased by 60 thousand tonnes at every price. Show the new supply schedule as $Q^{S'}$ on the previous table.

   a. The new equilibrium price of corn is $_____ per tonne.

   b. The new equilibrium quantity of corn is _____ thousand tonnes.

   c. Has the demand for corn changed as a result of this change in supply? Explain briefly. _____
   _____
   _____

3. Give an example of a factor that could have caused such an increase in the supply of corn, and explain briefly. _____
   _____
   _____
   _____

4. Notice that the increase in supply has resulted in a lower price and a higher quantity. Does this violate the Law of Supply, which states that the quantity supplied of a good increases as its price increases, all else being equal? Explain briefly. _____
   _____
   _____
   _____
   _____
   _____

The Market for Corn

Price of Corn
(dollars per tonne)

Quantity of Corn
(thousands of tonnes)

E. Advanced Critical Thinking

Consider the following editorial that appeared in a leading U.S. business publication following a freeze that destroyed much of the coffee crop in the late 1970s:

Coffee prices, it seems, are coming down again, after hitting a record high of $4.42 last year. An Agriculture Department economist, who had predicted $5-a-pound coffee this year, says he "underestimated the power of the U.S. consumer movement." Perhaps, or maybe, as with so many economists these days, he simply forgot his freshman economics, which has nothing to do with "movements." The coffee market is behaving the way the basic textbooks say a market behaves: Prices go up, demand falls, and prices come down.

— The Wall Street Journal, *November 30, 1977*

1. Suppose that coffee had started out at an equilibrium price of $1.00 per pound prior to the freeze.

    a. Show graphically the initial equilibrium, labelling supply and demand as S_1 and D_1 respectively. Use Q_1 to identify the original equilibrium quantity.

    _____

    _____

    b. Show graphically the effect of a freeze that destroys much of the coffee crop, labelling the new supply as S_2 and the new equilibrium quantity as Q_2. (The new equilibrium price is $4.42.) _____

    _____

    _____

    _____

    c. Does the answer to part (b) show a change in demand? Why or why not?

    _____

    _____

    _____

    d. Based on your analysis in parts (a–c), critique the *Wall Street Journal* editorial. What's wrong with its analysis? _____

    _____

    _____

    _____

    _____

III. Solutions

A. True/False Questions

1. F; quantity demanded, not demand, will increase.
2. T
3. T
4. F; technology tends to *increase* the supply (shift it to the right) by increasing productivity; that is, increasing output per unit of input.
5. T
6. T
7. F; the goods offered for sale are all exactly the same.
8. F; price below equilibrium results in excess demand, as buyers try to buy more than sellers are willing to sell at the low price.
9. T
10. F; increased supply moves the equilibrium to the right along the demand curve, resulting in a higher quantity and a lower price.
11. F; an increase in both supply and demand will increase equilibrium quantity, but the effect on price depends on which curve shifts more; if they shift equally, price remains unchanged.
12. T
13. T
14. T
15. F; a decrease in the price of a good tends to decrease the demand for its substitutes.

B. Multiple-Choice Questions

1. a	5. c	9. d	13. d	17. c
2. d	6. a	10. a	14. b	18. d
3. c	7. d	11. a	15. a	19. b
4. c	8. b	12. d	16. b	20. c

C. Short-Answer Questions

1. An increase in consumer income increases the demand for normal goods and decreases the demand for inferior goods.

2. Prices of other goods are held constant in deriving a demand curve, even though they can affect consumption. When they change, the demand also changes (shifts right or left). The price of the good itself does not shift the demand, however, because price is already built into our definition of demand. Demand for a good includes all the quantities that consumers are willing to buy at various prices of the good, thus holding other factors constant.

3. The goods offered for sale are all exactly the same and no single buyer or seller has any influence over the price.

4. income, prices of related goods, tastes, expectations, and number of buyers

5. input prices, technology, expectations, and number of sellers

D. Practice Problems

1. a. $4.50 per tonne

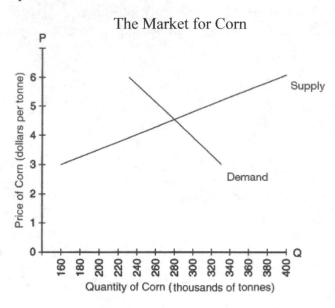

The Market for Corn

b. 280 thousand tonnes

c. shortage; 180 thousand tonnes; rise

d. surplus; 60 thousand tonnes; fall

2.

Price	Q^D	Q^S	$Q^{S'}$
$6.00	220	400	460
$5.50	240	360	420
$5.00	260	320	380
$4.50	280	280	340
$4.00	300	240	300
$3.50	320	200	260
$3.00	340	160	220

a. $4.00 per tonne

b. 300 thousand tonnes

c. Demand has not changed. Supply increased, thus moving the equilibrium along the existing demand curve to a higher quantity and lower price.

3.   Any of the factors that lower cost of production could shift the supply to the right, indicating increased willingness to sell at each price. For example, improvements in technology that increase productivity would lower cost and increase the supply.

4.   No, this does not violate the Law of Supply. The Law of Supply holds other factors, such as technology, constant. The increase in supply represents a new supply curve, with an increased *willingness to sell*. Both the old and the new supply curves follow the Law of Supply: as long as those other factors are constant, sellers will tend to be willing to sell more, but only at a higher price.

E. Advanced Critical Thinking

1.   a.   The original equilibrium should be at a price of $1.00, with the quantity simply labelled Q_1.

      b.   The new equilibrium should be at a price of $4.42 and a quantity of Q_2, after a leftward shift in supply and a movement along the (unchanged) demand curve. Equilibrium price is higher and quantity is lower.

      c.   Demand did not change; only the quantity demanded changed as the supply shifted left, thus moving along the existing demand curve. There were no changes in the factors that are held constant in deriving a demand curve.

      d.   The newspaper's analysis was flawed. They confused (shifts in) demand with simple changes in quantity demanded in response to a price change. For the price to fall, one of the factors (other than price) affecting either supply or demand must have changed.

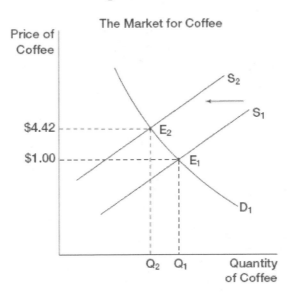

NEL

IV. APPENDIX: The Mathematics of Market Equilibrium

1. Suppose that the demand function for pizza is given by $Q^D = 70 - 4P$ and that the supply function for pizza is given by $Q^S = -20 + 5P$. Which one of the following describes the equilibrium price and quantity of pizza?
    a. $P = \$10; Q = 10$
    b. $P = \$10; Q = 30$
    c. $P = \$30; Q = 10$
    d. $P = \$30; Q = 30$

2. Suppose now that the price of hamburgers increases and, as a result, the demand for pizza increases to $Q^D = 88 - 4P$. Which one of the following describes the new equilibrium price and quantity of pizza?
    a. $P = \$10; Q = 30$
    b. $P = \$10; Q = 40$
    c. $P = \$12; Q = 30$
    d. $P = \$12; Q = 40$

3. Suppose that the supply function for laptop computers is given by $Q^S = 1000 + 2P$, and that the demand function for laptop computers is given by $Q^D = 4000 - 3P$. Which one of the following describes the equilibrium price and quantity of laptop computers?
    a. $P = \$600; Q = 600$
    b. $P = \$600; Q = 2200$
    c. $P = \$800; Q = 600$
    d. $P = \$800; Q = 2200$

4. Suppose now that there is an improvement in technology in the production of laptop computers and, as a result, the supply of laptop computers increases to $Q^S = 2000 + 2P$. Which one of the following describes the new equilibrium price and quantity of laptop computers?
    a. $P = \$400; Q = 2200$
    b. $P = \$400; Q = 2800$
    c. $P = \$600; Q = 2200$
    d. $P = \$600; Q = 2800$

5. Suppose that the supply function for apples is given by $Q^S = 900 + 30P$. Which one of the following demand functions will result in an equilibrium price for apples of $2 per kilogram?
    a. $Q^D = 800 - 10P$
    b. $Q^D = 800 - 20P$
    c. $Q^D = 900 - 10P$
    d. $Q^D = 1000 - 20P$

V. Solutions for Appendix

1. b
2. d
3. b
4. b
5. d

5 Measuring a Nation's Income

I. Chapter Overview

A. Context and Purpose

Chapter 5 is the first chapter in the macroeconomics section of the text. It is the first of a two-chapter sequence that introduces two vital statistics that economists use to monitor the economy: gross domestic product (GDP) and the consumer price index (CPI). Chapter 5 develops how economists measure expenditure and income in the economy; Chapter 6 develops how economists measure the level of prices in the economy. Taken together, Chapter 5 concentrates on the *quantity* of output in the economy, while Chapter 6 addresses *prices* in the economy.

The purpose of this chapter is to provide you with an understanding of the measurement and use of GDP. GDP is the single most important measure of the health of the economy. Indeed, it is the most widely reported statistic in every developed economy.

B. Helpful Hints

1. *GDP measures production.* In setting out to measure GDP, it is important to remember that it is *production* over a period of time that is being measured. By remembering that, correctly accounting for unusual types of production is generally achieved. Here are some examples:

   - How should the measurement of the production of a cruise ship that takes three years to build and is sold at the end of the third year be handled? Logically, the portion of the ship that was completed during each year should be counted and applied to that year's GDP. In fact, that is what economists do. If the entire ship had been accounted for in the year in which it was sold, the GDP would have been overestimated in the third year and underestimated in the previous two years.

   - Similarly, if a new house was built during one year but sold for the first time during the next year, it should be accounted for during the first year because that is when it was produced. That is, the builder "purchased" the finished home during the first year and added it to his or her inventory of homes.

     While, in general, economists wish to count only final goods and services, they do count the production of intermediate goods that were not used during the period but were added to a firm's inventory because this production will not be captured by counting all the final goods.

2. *GDP does not include all expenditures.* We have learned that we can measure GDP by adding the expenditures on final goods and services ($Y = C + I + G + NX$). After having learned the expenditure approach, however, do not forget the words "on final goods and services" and mistakenly count all expenditures. When expenditures on used items, intermediate goods, stocks and bonds, or government transfer payments are included, the dollar value is very large, but it has nothing to do with GDP. The dollar value of total transactions in the economy is enormous and many times that of GDP.

3. *Intermediate goods and final goods are distinct.* It should be helpful to clarify the distinction between intermediate goods and final goods with an example. Recall:

   - Intermediate goods are goods that are produced by one firm to be further processed by another firm.

   - Final goods are sold to the end user.

   GDP includes only the value of the final goods and services because the value of the intermediate goods used in the production of a final good or service is fully captured in the price of the final good or service. If the value of intermediate production is included in GDP, the intermediate goods would be double counted.

   If this distinction is understood, can the *items* in the economy that are intermediate or final be listed? For example, is a tire an intermediate good or a final good? The answer is, it depends on who bought it. When General Motors buys a tire from Goodyear, the tire is an intermediate good because General Motors will attach it to a car and sell that. When a person buys a tire from your Goodyear dealer, it is a final good and should be counted in GDP. Thus, it is difficult to list items in the economy that are intermediate or final without knowledge of the buyer.

4. *Comparisons of GDP across countries and time can be biased.* Be cautious when comparing GDP across nations of different levels of market development, and when comparing GDP across long periods of time within a single nation. This is because GDP excludes most nonmarket activities. Clearly, a greater proportion of the output of less-developed nations is likely to be household production, such as when someone does their own farming, cleaning, sewing, and maybe even home construction. Because these activities are not captured by a market transaction, they are not recorded in less-developed nations or in earlier periods of industrialized nations when market development was less extensive. This results in an even lower estimate of their GDP.

II. Self-Testing Challenges

A. True/False Questions

_____1. For an economy as a whole, income equals expenditure because the income of the seller must be equal to the expenditure of the buyer.

_____2. The production of an apple contributes more to GDP than the production of a gold ring because food is necessary for life itself.

_____3. If the lumber yard sells $1000 of lumber to a carpenter, and the carpenter uses the lumber to build a garage that he sells for $5000, the contribution to GDP is $6000.

_____4. A country with a larger GDP per person generally has a greater standard of living or quality of life than a country with a smaller GDP per person.

_____5. If nominal GDP in 2013 is less than nominal GDP in 2012, then real output must have fallen.

_____6. When a Canadian citizen works temporarily in the United States, her production is part of U.S. GDP.

_____7. Wages are an example of a transfer payment because there is a transfer of payment from the firm to the worker.

_____8. Since the mid-1990s, foreigners control more Canadian industry than Canadians control foreign industry.

_____9. Nominal GDP employs current prices to value output, while real GDP employs constant base-year prices to value output.

_____10. A new car produced in 2012, but first sold in 2013, should be counted in 2013 GDP because that is when it was first sold as a final good.

_____11. GNP measures the value of all income earned by Canadians, including income earned by Canadians in foreign countries.

_____12. A recession occurs when real GDP declines.

_____13. Investment spending includes household purchases of new housing.

_____14. The price of gasoline, $1.20 per litre, includes $0.30 per litre in taxes. Therefore, only $0.90 per litre should be included in GDP.

_____15. Net exports equal exports plus imports.

B. Multiple-Choice Questions

1. Which one of the following is an example of a transfer payment?
   a. Employment Insurance benefits
   b. wages
   c. profit
   d. rent

2. Which one of the following describes the purchase of plant and equipment by General Motors?
   a. The purchase is part of exports.
   b. The purchase is part of depreciation.
   c. The purchase is part of consumption.
   d. The purchase is part of investment.

3. Which one of the following would be excluded from 2013 GDP?
   a. The sale of a haircut.
   b. The sale of a realtor's services.
   c. The sale of a home built in 2012 and first sold in 2013.
   d. The sale of a 2013 Chrysler vehicle made in Windsor, Ontario.

4. Which one of the following explains how gross domestic product is measured?
   a. as the sum of consumption, transfer payments, wages, and profits
   b. as the sum of investment, wages, profits, and intermediate production
   c. as the sum of consumption, investment, government purchases, and net exports
   d. as the sum of final goods and services, intermediate goods, transfer payments, and rent

5. Which one of the following is measured by the Canadian Gross National Product?
   a. the production and income of the domestic service sector only
   b. the production and income of the domestic manufacturing sector only
   c. the production and income of people and factories located within the borders of Canada
   d. the production and income of Canadians and their factories, no matter where they are located in the world

6. Which one of the following defines gross domestic product?
   a. the sum of the market value of final goods and services
   b. the sum of the market value of normal goods and services
   c. the sum of the market value of intermediate goods
   d. the sum of the market value of manufactured goods

7. If nominal GDP in 2013 exceeds nominal GDP in 2012, which one of the following must have occurred in production of real output?
   a. It must have risen.
   b. It must have fallen.
   c. It must have stayed the same.
   d. It may have risen or fallen or stayed the same because there is not enough information to determine what happened to real output.

8. Suppose a cobbler buys leather for $100 and thread for $50 and uses them to produce and sell $500 worth of shoes to consumers. Which one of the following is the contribution to GDP?
   a. $150
   b. $350
   c. $500
   d. $650

9. Which one of the following would be included in GDP?
   a. housework
   b. illegal drug sales
   c. intermediate sales
   d. legal services

10. Real GDP is measured in _____ prices, while nominal GDP is measured in _____ prices.
    a. domestic; foreign
    b. intermediate; final
    c. base year; current year
    d. current year; base year

The following table contains information about an economy that produces only pens and books. The base year is 2011. Use this information for questions 11–16.

Year	Price of Pens	Quantity of Pens	Price of Books	Quantity of Books
2011	$3	100	$10	50
2012	$3	120	$12	70
2013	$4	120	$14	70

11. Which one of the following is the value of nominal GDP for 2012?
    a. $800
    b. $1060
    c. $1200
    d. $1460

12. Which one of the following is the value of real GDP for 2012?
    a. $800
    b. $1060
    c. $1200
    d. $1460

13. Which one of the following is the value of the GDP deflator in 2012?
    a. 100
    b. 113
    c. 116
    d. 119

14. Which one of the following is the percentage increase in prices from 2011 to 2012?
    a. 0 percent
    b. 13 percent
    c. 16 percent
    d. 19 percent

15. Which one of the following is the percentage increase in real GDP from 2011 to 2012?
    a. 0 percent
    b. 13 percent
    c. 23 percent
    d. 33 percent

16. Which one of the following is the percentage increase in real GDP from 2012 to 2013?
    a. 0 percent
    b. 7 percent
    c. 22 percent
    d. 27 percent

17. Which one of the following is included in GDP?
    a. volunteer work
    b. medical services
    c. leisure
    d. quality of the environment

18. Which one of the following is NOT included in Canadian GDP?
    a. grapes purchased by a Niagara winery
    b. legal services purchased by a homebuyer
    c. lawn care services purchased by a homeowner
    d. a new bridge purchased by the province of Prince Edward Island

19. Suppose Jane purchases a $60 000 BMW that was produced in Germany. Which one of the following describes how this would be recorded in the Canadian GDP accounts?
    a. Net exports increase by $60 000.
    b. Net exports decrease by $60 000.
    c. Investment increases by $60 000, and net exports increase by $60 000.
    d. Consumption increases by $60 000, and net exports decrease by $60 000.

20. Which one of the following will be affected when a person purchases a new home?
    a. investment
    b. net exports
    c. consumption
    d. government purchases

C. Short-Answer Questions

1. Why does income = expenditure = GDP? _____
   _____
   _____

2. Define GDP and explain the important terms in the definition.
   _____
   _____
   _____
   _____

3. What are the components of expenditure? Provide an example of each.
   _____
   _____
   _____

4. Provide an example of a transfer payment. Is it included in GDP? Why or why not? _____
   _____
   _____

5. GDP is not a perfect measure of economic well-being. What factors that contribute to a good life are left out of GDP? _____
   _____
   _____

6. If real GDP in 2013 exceeds real GDP in 2012, did real output rise? Did prices rise? _____
   _____
   _____

7. If a Canadian buys a $35 000 Toyota that was produced fully in Japan, does this affect Canadian GDP? Show how this transaction would affect the appropriate expenditure categories that make up GDP. _____

_____

_____

8. In the year 2011, what was the approximate value of Canadian GDP per person? What component of GDP is the largest? _____

_____

_____

_____

9. Which contributes more to the measurement of GDP, a new diamond necklace purchased by a wealthy person, or a soft drink purchased by a thirsty person? Why? _____

_____

10. If Serena hires someone to mow her lawn instead of doing it herself, what will happen to GDP? Why? Did output change? _____

_____

_____

D. Practice Problems

1. a. Complete the following table. The data are in millions of dollars.

	Year 1	Year 2	Year 3
Gross domestic product	4532	4804	_____
Consumption	_____	3320	3544
Investment	589	629	673
Government purchases	861	_____	977
Net exports	−45	−58	−54

   b. What is the largest expenditure component of GDP? _____

_____

   c. Does investment include the purchase of stocks and bonds? Why or why not?

_____

_____

_____

_____

   d. Does the "government purchases" component include government spending on Employment Insurance benefits? Why or why not? _____

_____

e. What does it mean when it is said that net exports are negative?

_____

_____

2. Suppose the base year in the following table is 2011.

Year	Production of X	Price per unit of X
2011	20 units	$5
2012	20 units	$10
2013	20 units	$20

a. What is nominal GDP for 2011, 2012, and 2013? _____

_____

b. What is real GDP for 2011, 2012, and 2013? _____

_____

3. Suppose the following table records the total output and prices for an entire economy. Further, suppose the base year in the following table is 2012.

Year	Price of soft drink	Quantity of soft drink	Price of pizza	Quantity of pizza
2012	$1.00	200	$10.00	50
2013	$1.00	220	$11.00	50

a. What is the value of nominal GDP in 2012? _____

b. What is the value of real GDP in 2012? _____

c. What is the value of nominal GDP in 2013? _____

d. What is the value of real GDP in 2013? _____

e. What is the value of the GDP deflator in 2012? _____

f. What is the value of the GDP deflator in 2013? _____

g. From 2012 to 2013, prices rose by approximately what percentage?

_____

h. Was the increase in nominal GDP from 2012 to 2013 due mostly to an increase in real output or to an increase in prices? _____

_____

_____

4.   Complete the following table:

Year	Nominal GDP	Real GDP	GDP deflator
1	——	$100	100
2	$120	——	120
3	$150	$125	——

a. What year is the base year? Explain why? _____
_____

b. From year 1 to year 2, did real output rise or did prices rise? Explain.
_____

c. From year 2 to year 3, did real output rise or did prices rise? Explain.
_____

E. Advanced Critical Thinking

Sean is watching a news report with his father. The news anchor points out that a certain troubled Caribbean nation generates a GDP per person of only $5000 Canadian per year. Because Sean's father knows GDP in Canada is approximately $50 000 Canadian per person, he suggests that Canadians are materially 10 times better off in Canada than in the Caribbean nation.

1.   Is the father's statement accurate? _____

2.   What general category of production is not captured by GDP in both Canada and the Caribbean nation? _____

3.   Provide some examples of this type of activity. _____
_____
_____

4.   Why would the exclusion of this type of production affect the measurement of Caribbean output more than Canadian output? _____
_____
_____

5.   Does this mean that residents of the Caribbean nation are actually as well off materially as residents in Canada? _____
_____
_____

III. Solutions

A. True/False Questions

1. T
2. F; contribution is based on market value.
3. F; the garage is the final good, valued at $5000.
4. T
5. F; prices or real output could have fallen.
6. T
7. F; transfer payments are expenditures for which no good or service is received in return.
8. F; Canadians control more foreign industry than foreigners control Canadian industry.
9. T
10. F; goods are counted in the year produced.
11. T
12. T
13. T
14. F; indirect taxes are included in GDP.
15. F; $NX = X - M$.

B. Multiple-Choice Questions

1. a	5. d	9. d	13. b	17. b
2. d	6. a	10. c	14. b	18. a
3. c	7. d	11. c	15. d	19. d
4. c	8. c	12. b	16. a	20. a

C. Short-Answer Questions

1. The income of the seller equals the expenditure of the buyer, and GDP can be measured with either one.

2. GDP is the market value of all final goods and services produced within a country in a given period of time. Market value (price paid) of all (all legal production) final (to end users) goods and services (includes services) produced (no used items) within a country (inside its borders) in a given period (per quarter or year).

3. consumption (food); investment (factory); government purchases (military equipment); net exports (sale of wheat to Japan minus purchase of wine from Germany)

4. Social assistance payments are an example of a transfer payment. No, because the government received no good or service in return.

5.   GDP excludes leisure, value of goods and services produced at home, volunteer work, quality of the environment, and distribution of income.

6.   Real output rose because the value of output in each year is measured in constant base year prices. There is no information on prices.

7.   No, consumption would increase by $35 000 and net exports would decrease by $35 000. As a result, Canadian GDP is unaffected.

8.   GDP per person, or the amount of expenditure for the average Canadian, was about $50 200 per year. Consumption made up about 57 percent of GDP, or about $28 700 per person.

9.   A diamond necklace contributes more to the measurement of GDP because GDP measures market value.

10.   GDP will rise because the mowing of the lawn now becomes a market transaction. However, output did not really rise.

D. Practice Problems

1.   a.

	Year 1	Year 2	Year 3
Gross domestic product	4532	4804	5140
Consumption	3127	3320	3544
Investment	589	629	673
Government purchases	861	913	977
Net exports	−45	−58	−54

Note: in millions of dollars

b. consumption

c. No, that transaction is a purchase of a financial asset, not a purchase of currently produced capital goods.

d. No, Employment Insurance benefits are expenditures for which the government receives no production in return.

e. It means that imports exceed exports.

2.   a. $100, $200, $400

b. $100, $100, $100

3. a. $700

    b. $700

    c. $770

    d. $720

    e. 100

    f. 107

    g. $(107 - 100)/100 = 0.07 = 7\%$

    h. Percent increase in nominal GDP ($770 – $700)/700 = 0.10 = 10%. Percent increase in prices = 7%; therefore, most of the increase was due to prices.

4.

Year	Nominal GDP	Real GDP	GDP deflator
1	$100	$100	100
2	$120	$100	120
3	$150	$125	120

    a. Year 1: the GDP deflator = 100.

    b. Prices rose 20 percent and real output stayed the same.

    c. Prices stayed the same and real output rose 25 percent.

E. Advanced Critical Thinking

1. no

2. nonmarket activities

3. household production done without pay by an individual, such as gardening, cleaning, sewing, home improvement or construction, child supervision, etc.

4. A greater proportion of the output produced by less-developed nations is nonmarket output; that is, it is not sold and recorded as a market transaction.

5. No; it just means that quantitative comparisons between nations of greatly different levels of development are very difficult and often inaccurate.

6 Measuring the Cost of Living

I. Chapter Overview

A. Context and Purpose

Chapter 6 is the second chapter of a two-chapter sequence that deals with how economists measure output and prices in the economy. Chapter 5 addressed how economists measure output; Chapter 6 develops how economists measure the overall price level in the economy.

The purpose of Chapter 6 is twofold: first, to show how to generate a price index, and second, to explain how to employ a price index to compare dollar figures from different points in time and to adjust interest rates for inflation. In addition, some of the shortcomings of using the consumer price index as a measure of the cost of living are explained.

B. Helpful Hints

1. *A person's particular consumption basket may not be typical.* Because the gross domestic product (GDP) deflator and the consumer price index (CPI) are based on different baskets of goods and services, each will provide a slightly different measurement of the cost of living. Continuing in this same line of thinking, a person's particular consumption basket may differ from the typical consumption basket used by Statistics Canada when it calculates the CPI. For example, the consumption basket of a young adult may be more heavily weighted toward electronics and clothing. If clothing prices are rising faster than average, young people may have a greater increase in the cost of living than is suggested by the CPI. In like manner, the consumption basket of an elderly person may be more heavily weighted toward home-care medical services and travel. Above-average increases in these prices may cause the cost of living for the elderly to rise more quickly than suggested by the CPI.

2. *Dollar values can be adjusted backward in time as well as forward.* For example, suppose Karen earned an income of $20 000 in 1990 and $36 000 in 2012.

    The CPI in 1990 (base year 2002) was 78.4, and the CPI in 2012 was 121.7. Karen's 1990 salary can be converted into 2012 dollars as follows:

    $$\$20\ 000 \times (121.7/78.4) = \$31\ 046$$

    Her $20 000 salary in 1990 would buy as much as a $31 046 salary in 2012. Because Karen earned $36 000 in 2012, her real income and standard of living rose over those 22 years.

Alternatively, Karen's 2012 salary can be converted into 1990 dollars as follows:

$$\$36\,000 \times (78.4/121.7) = \$23\,191$$

Karen's $36 000 salary in 2012 would buy as much as a $23 191 salary in 1990. Because she earned $20 000 in 1990, Karen's real income and standard of living were higher in 2012.

3. *When correcting interest rates for inflation, think like a lender.* If Karen loans someone $100 for one year, and she charges 7 percent interest, she will receive $107 at the end of the year. Did Karen receive 7 additional dollars of purchasing power? Suppose inflation was 4 percent. She would need to receive $104 at the end of the year just to break even. That is, Karen would need $104 just to be able to buy the same set of goods and services that she could have purchased for $100 at the time she granted the loan. In this sense, Karen received only three additional dollars of purchasing power for having made the $100 loan, or a 3 percent real return. Thus, the *real interest rate* on the loan is 3 percent, using the formula

$$7\% - 4\% = 3\%$$

Although not explicitly stated, the interest rate example in the text is also approached from the lender's perspective. That is, when a person deposits money in a bank and receives interest, the deposit is actually a loan from the depositor to the bank.

II. Self-Testing Challenges

A. True/False Questions

_____ 1. An increase in the price of imported cameras is captured by the CPI but not by the GDP deflator.

_____ 2. An increase in the price of helicopters purchased by the Canadian military is captured by the CPI.

_____ 3. Because an increase in gasoline prices causes consumers to ride their bikes more and drive their cars less, the CPI tends to underestimate the cost of living.

_____ 4. An increase in the price of diamonds will have a greater impact on the CPI than an equal percentage increase in the price of food because diamonds are so much more expensive.

_____ 5. The rate of core inflation excludes the most volatile components from the CPI basket.

_____ 6. If the CPI rises at 5 percent per year, then every individual in the country needs exactly a 5 percent increase in their income for their standard of living to remain constant.

_____ 7. The GDP deflator is constructed to measure the change in price of domestically produced goods and services.

_____ 8. If Statistics Canada fails to recognize that recently produced automobiles can be driven for many more kilometres than older models, then the CPI tends to overestimate the cost of living.

_____ 9. If a worker's hourly wage rises from $11.50 to $13.10, while the CPI rises from 103 to 122, the worker should feel an increase in standard of living.

_____ 10. The largest category of goods and services in the CPI is transportation.

_____ 11. It is impossible for _real_ interest rates to be negative.

_____ 12. If the nominal interest rate is 12 percent and the rate of inflation is 7 percent, then the real rate of interest is 5 percent.

_____ 13. If lenders demand a real rate of return of 4 percent and they expect inflation to be 5 percent, then they should charge 9 percent interest when they extend loans.

_____ 14. If borrowers and lenders agree on a nominal interest rate, and inflation turns out to be greater than they had anticipated, lenders will gain at the expense of borrowers.

_____ 15. If workers and firms agree on an increase in wages based on their expectations of inflation, and inflation turns out to be less than they expected, workers will gain at the expense of firms.

B. Multiple-Choice Questions

1. Which one of the following is a measure of inflation?
    a. GDP deflator
    b. nominal GDP
    c. real GDP
    d. real rate of interest

2. Which one of the following would have the **MOST** influence on CPI?
    a. a 10 percent increase in the price of food
    b. a 10 percent increase in the price of shelter
    c. a 10 percent increase in the price of transportation
    d. a 10 percent increase in the price of health and personal care

3. In 2011, the CPI was 119.9. In 2012, it was 121.7. Which one of the following was the rate of inflation for 2012?
    a. 1.5 percent
    b. 1.8 percent
    c. 2.2 percent
    d. 2.5 percent

4. Which one of the following would cause the CPI to rise more than the GDP deflator?
    a. an increase in the price of agricultural machinery
    b. an increase in the price of tanks purchased by the military
    c. an increase in the price of Hondas produced in Japan and sold in Canada
    d. an increase in the price of domestically produced telecommunications equipment sold exclusively to the United States

5. Which one of the following describes the composition of the "basket" on which the CPI is based?
    a. consumer production
    b. total current production
    c. raw materials purchased by firms
    d. products purchased by the typical consumer

6. Suppose there is an increase in the price of apples that causes consumers to purchase fewer kilograms of apples and more kilograms of oranges. Which one of the following will the CPI suffer from?
    a. base-year bias
    b. commodity substitution bias
    c. bias due to unmeasured quality change
    d. bias due to the introduction of new goods

Use the following table for questions 7–12. The table shows the prices and the quantities consumed in Carnivore Country. The base year is 2011. (This is also the year the typical consumption basket was determined.)

Year	Price of beef	Quantity of beef	Price of chicken	Quantity of chicken
2011	$2.00	100	$1.00	100
2012	$2.50	90	$0.90	120
2013	$2.75	105	$1.00	130

7. Which one of the following is the value of the basket in the base year?
    a. $300
    b. $333
    c. $418.75
    d. $459.25

8. Which one of the following lists the values of the CPI in 2011, 2012, and 2013, respectively?
    a. 100, 111, 139.6
    b. 100, 109.2, 116
    c. 100, 113.3, 125
    d. 83.5, 94.2, 100

9. Which one of the following is the inflation rate for 2012?
    a. 0 percent
    b. 9.2 percent
    c. 11 percent
    d. 13.3 percent

10. Which one of the following is the inflation rate for 2013?
    a. 0 percent
    b. 10.3 percent
    c. 11 percent
    d. 13.3 percent

11. Which one of the following explains why the table shows that the 2012 inflation rate is biased upward?
    a. base-year bias
    b. commodity substitution bias
    c. bias due to unmeasured quality change
    d. bias due to the introduction of new goods

12.   Suppose the base year is changed in the table from 2011 to 2013 (now use the 2013 consumption basket). Which one of the following is the new value of the CPI in 2012?
a. 80.6
b. 88.6
c. 90.6
d. 100.0

13.   Suppose Peter's income rises from $46 000 to $59 000, while the CPI rises from 107 to 158. Which one of the following has likely occurred to Peter's standard of living?
a. It has likely fallen.
b. It has likely risen.
c. It has likely stayed the same.

14.   If the nominal interest rate is 7 percent and the inflation rate is 3 percent, which one of the following is the real interest rate?
a. −4 percent
b. 3 percent
c. 4 percent
d. 10 percent

15.   Which one of the following statements is correct?
a. The real interest rate is the sum of the nominal interest rate and the inflation rate.
b. The real interest rate is the nominal interest rate minus the inflation rate.
c. The nominal interest rate is the inflation rate minus the real interest rate.
d. The nominal interest rate is the real interest rate minus the inflation rate.

16.   If expected inflation is 3 percent and the real interest rate is 2 percent, then which one of the following should be the nominal interest rate?
a. 1 percent
b. 3 percent
c. 5 percent
d. 6 percent

17.   Which one of the following describes conditions under which it is preferable to be the lender?
a. The nominal rate of interest is 20 percent and the inflation rate is 25 percent.
b. The nominal rate of interest is 15 percent and the inflation rate is 14 percent.
c. The nominal rate of interest is 12 percent and the inflation rate is 9 percent.
d. The nominal rate of interest is 5 percent and the inflation rate is 1 percent.

18. Which one of the following describes conditions under which it is preferable to be the borrower?
   a. The nominal rate of interest is 20 percent and the inflation rate is 25 percent.
   b. The nominal rate of interest is 15 percent and the inflation rate is 14 percent.
   c. The nominal rate of interest is 12 percent and the inflation rate is 9 percent.
   d. The nominal rate of interest is 5 percent and the inflation rate is 1 percent.

19. Which one of the following will occur if borrowers and lenders agree on a nominal interest rate, and inflation turns out to be less than they had expected?
   a. Borrowers will gain at the expense of lenders.
   b. Lenders will gain at the expense of borrowers.
   c. Neither borrowers nor lenders will gain because the nominal interest rate has been fixed by contract.

20. Which one of the following will occur if workers and firms agree on an increase in wages based on their expectations of inflation, and inflation turns out to be more than they expected?
   a. Firms will gain at the expense of workers.
   b. Workers will gain at the expense of firms.
   c. Neither workers nor firms will gain because the increase in wages is fixed in the labour agreement.

C. Short-Answer Questions

1. What does the consumer price index attempt to measure?_____
   _____

2. What are the steps that one must go through in order to construct a consumer price index? _____
   _____
   _____

3. Which would have a greater impact on the CPI: a 20 percent increase in the price of Rolex watches, or a 20 percent increase in the price of new cars? Why?
   _____

4. Suppose there is an increase in the price of BMW automobiles imported from Germany. Would this have a larger impact on the CPI or the GDP deflator? Why?
   _____
   _____

5. If Statistics Canada failed to recognize the increase in memory, power, and speed of newer model computers, in which direction would the CPI be biased? What is this type of bias called? _____
   _____   _____

6.   What does the real interest rate measure? _____

_____

7.   Suppose Melvin lends money to his sister at a nominal interest rate of 10 percent because they both expect the inflation rate to be 6 percent. Further, suppose that after the loan has been repaid, Melvin discovers that the actual inflation rate over the life of the loan was only 2 percent. Who gained at the other's expense: Melvin or his sister? Why? _____

_____

_____

8.   Paying close attention to Question 7, make a general statement with respect to who gains or loses (the borrower or the lender) on a loan contract when inflation turns out to be either higher or lower than expected. _____

_____

_____

9.   If workers and firms negotiate a wage increase based on their expectation of inflation, who gains or loses (the workers or the firms) if actual inflation turns out to be higher than expected? Why? _____

_____

10.   There are 3 measurement problems with the CPI: commodity substitution bias; introduction of new goods; and unmeasured quality change. What is the estimated impact of these biases on the Canadian CPI? _____

_____

_____

D.   Practice Problems

1.   The following table shows the prices and quantities consumed in the country known as College Canada. Suppose the base year is 2011. (This is also the year the typical consumption basket was determined.)

Year	Price of books	Quantity of books	Price of pencils	Quantity of pencils	Price of pens	Quantity of pens
2011	$50	10	$1	100	$5	100
2012	$50	12	$1	200	$10	50
2013	$60	12	$1.50	250	$20	20

a.   What is the value of the CPI in 2011? _____

_____

b.   What is the value of the CPI in 2012? _____

_____

c.   What is the value of the CPI in 2013? _____

_____

d.   What is the inflation rate in 2012? _____

_____

e.   What is the inflation rate in 2013? _____

_____

f.   What type of bias do you observe in the CPI and corresponding inflation rates you generated above? Explain. _____

_____

_____

g.   If workers had a COLA clause in their wage contract based on the CPI calculated above, would their standard of living likely increase, decrease, or stay the same over the years 2011–2013? Why? _____

_____

h.   If Davis personally consumes only pens (no books or pencils), would his standard of living likely increase, decrease, or stay the same over the years 2011–2013? Why? _____

_____

_____

2.   The following table contains the CPI (base year 2002) and the average hourly earnings of Canadian workers for the period 2000–2012.

Year	CPI	Average hourly earnings ($)
2000	95.4	16.49
2001	97.8	16.78
2002	100.0	17.08
2003	102.8	17.20
2004	104.7	17.73
2005	107.0	18.30
2006	109.1	18.76
2007	111.5	19.48
2008	114.1	20.16
2009	114.4	20.44
2010	116.5	20.96
2011	119.9	21.76
2012	121.7	22.28

a. Inflate the 2000 average hourly earnings to its equivalent value measured in 2012 prices. _____

_____

b. What happened to real average hourly earnings over this 12-year period?

_____

c. Deflate the 2012 average hourly earnings to its equivalent value measured in 2000 prices. _____

_____

d. Do these two methods provide consistent answers with respect to real average hourly earnings over this 12-year period? _____

_____

_____

3.   Suppose that Yolanda lends her roommate $100 for one year at 9 percent nominal interest.

a. How many dollars of interest will the roommate pay Yolanda at the end of the year? _____

b. Suppose that, at the time they agreed to the terms of the loan, they both expected the inflation rate to be 5 percent during the year of the loan. What do they both expect the real interest rate to be on the loan?

_____

c. Suppose that, at the end of the year, Yolanda is surprised to discover that the actual inflation rate over the year was 8 percent. What was the actual real interest rate generated by this loan? _____

_____

d. In the case described above, actual inflation turned out to be higher than expected. Who had the unexpected gain or loss: the roommate (the borrower) or Yolanda (the lender)? Why? _____

_____

_____

e. What would the real interest rate on the loan have been if the actual inflation rate had turned out to be a whopping 11 percent? _____

_____

f. Explain what it means to have a negative real interest rate. _____

_____

_____

E. Advanced Critical Thinking

Joan's father stopped drinking beer in 2005. When she asked him why he stopped, he said, "I stopped because it was just getting too expensive. In 1990, beer was only $24.00 per case. The last case I bought in 2005 was $32.00, and I just couldn't justify spending $8.00 more on a case of beer."

1. In 1990 the CPI was 78.4. In 2005 the CPI was 107.0. What is wrong with his explanation? _____

_____

_____

2. What is the equivalent cost of a 1990 case of beer measured in 2005 prices?

_____

3. What is the equivalent cost of a 2005 case of beer measured in 1990 prices?

_____

4. Do both methods provide the same conclusion? _____

_____

_____

5. The preceding example demonstrates what economists refer to as "money illusion." Why would economists choose the phrase "money illusion" to describe this behaviour? _____

_____

_____

III. Solutions

A. True/False Questions

1.   T
2.   F; military helicopters are not consumer goods.
3.   F; the CPI tends to overstate the cost of living because people substitute toward cheaper goods.
4.   F; prices in the CPI are weighted according to how much consumers buy of each, and food is a larger portion of the consumption basket.
5.   T
6.   F; the CPI tends to overstate the effects of inflation.
7.   T
8.   T
9.   F; wages increased by 13.9%, while prices increased by 18.4%.
10.   F; the largest category is shelter.
11.   F; if inflation exceeds the nominal interest rate, the real interest rate is negative.
12.   T
13.   T
14.   F; borrowers will gain at the expense of lenders.
15.   T

B. Multiple-Choice Questions

1. a	5. d	9. d	13. a	17. d
2. b	6. b	10. b	14. c	18. a
3. a	7. a	11. b	15. b	19. b
4. c	8. c	12. c	16. c	20. a

C. Short-Answer Questions

1.   the overall cost of the goods and services purchased by the typical consumer

2.   Determine the basket, find the prices, compute the basket's cost, choose a base year, and compute the index; use the index to calculate the inflation rate.

3.   new cars, because they have a greater weight in the typical consumption basket

4.   the CPI, because BMWs are in the typical consumption basket, but BMWs are not included in Canadian GDP

5.   upward, unmeasured quality change

6.   the nominal interest rate adjusted for the effects of inflation

7. Expected real interest rate = 4%; actual real interest rate = 8%. Melvin gained and his sister lost.

8. When inflation is higher than expected, borrowers gain; when inflation is lower than expected, lenders gain.

9. Firms gain and workers lose because wages did not rise as much as the cost of living.

10. It is estimated that the Canadian CPI overstates the true cost of living by about 0.6 percentage points per year.

D. Practice Problems

1. a. ($1100/$1100) $\times$ 100 = 100

   b. ($1600/$1100) $\times$ 100 = 145.5

   c. ($2750/$1100) $\times$ 100 = 250

   d. (145.5 − 100)/100 = 0.455 = 45.5%

   e. (250 − 145.5)/145.5 = 0.718 = 71.8%

   f. Commodity substitution bias, because as the price of pens increased, the quantity consumed declined significantly.

   g. Increase, because this CPI overstates the increase in the cost of living.

   h. Decrease, because the price of pens has increased by a greater percentage than the CPI.

2. a. $16.49 $\times$ (121.7/95.4) = $21.04

   b. They increased slightly because $22.28 > $21.04.

   c. $22.28 $\times$ (95.4/121.7) = $17.47

   d. Yes, because $17.47 > $16.49. Real average hourly earnings are slightly higher in 2012 compared to 2000.

3. a. $9

   b. 9% − 5% = 4%

   c. 9% − 8% = 1%

d. The roommate (the borrower) gained and Yolanda lost because the borrower repaid the loan with dollars of unexpectedly lower purchasing power.

e. $9\% - 11\% = -2\%$

f. Because of inflation, the nominal interest payment is not large enough, so the lender loses purchasing power compared to the day the loan was made.

E. Advanced Critical Thinking

1. Joan's father is only looking at the price of beer uncorrected for inflation. The real cost of beer has not risen as much as it first appears.

2. $\$24.00 \times (107.0/78.4) = \$32.76$

3. $\$32.00 \times (78.4/107.0) = \$23.45$

4. Yes, each method suggests that, after correcting for inflation, beer was actually more expensive in 1990.

5. When people base decisions on money values uncorrected for inflation, there may be an illusion that the cost of living has risen.

I. Chapter Overview

A. Context and Purpose

Chapter 7 is the first chapter in a three-chapter sequence about the production of output in the long run. Chapter 7 addresses the determinants of the level and the growth rate of output. Chapter 8 addresses the market for investment in capital. Chapter 9 examines the labour market.

The purpose of Chapter 7 is to examine the long-run determinants of both the level and the growth rate of real GDP per person. Along the way, we will discover the factors that determine the productivity of workers and address what governments might do to improve the productivity of their citizens.

B. Helpful Hints

1. *Compound growth is the same as compound interest.* Compound interest is interest earned on your previously earned interest. Assuming annual compounding, when you deposit $100 in a bank account with an interest rate of 10 percent, you will have $110 at the end of the year. If you leave the $110 in the account two years, the interest will compound and you will have $121 at the end of two years—the $100 principal, $10 interest from the first year, $10 interest from the second year, *plus $1 interest on the first year's $10 interest earned.* At the end of the next year, interest would be earned not on $100, or $110, but on $121, and so on. In a like manner, after a number of years, a faster growing economy is applying its percentage growth rate to a much larger base (size of economy), while total output accelerates away from economies that are growing more slowly.

2. *An old rule of thumb, called the rule of 70, says that if some variable grows at a rate of x percent per year, then that variable doubles in approximately 70/x years.* For example, an economy that is growing at 1 percent should double in size after about 70 years (70/1). An economy growing at 4 percent should double in size every 17.5 years (70/4). After 70 years, the 4 percent growth economy is 16 times its original size, while the 1 percent growth economy is only twice its original size. If both economies started at the same size, the 4 percent growth economy is now eight times the size of the 1 percent growth economy because of compound growth.

3. *A simple example more clearly defines the factors of production.* The simpler the production process, the easier it is to separate and analyze the factors of production. For example, suppose output is "number of holes dug in the ground." Then the production function is as follows:

$$Y = A F (L, K, H, N)$$

where Y is number of holes dug, A is technological knowledge, L is labour, K is physical capital, H is human capital, N is natural resources, and F is a mathematical function that relates how the inputs are combined to produce output. If we have more workers, there is an increase in L, and Y would increase. If we have more shovels, there is an increase in K, and Y would increase. If workers are educated such that more of them dig with the spaded end of the shovel rather than digging with the handle, there is an increase in H, and Y would increase (but note that the number of workers and the number of shovels are unchanged). If our country has softer soil such that digging is easier here, N is larger and therefore Y is larger. Finally, if we discover that it is more productive to dig after it rains rather than during a drought, there is an increase in A, and Y should increase.

II. Self-Testing Challenges

A. True/False Questions

_____1.   The U.S. economy should grow faster than that of Canada because the United States has a larger economy.

_____2.   Growth accumulates over time because of compounding.

_____3.   Rising prices for natural resources demonstrate that natural resources are a limit to economic growth.

_____4.   Human capital refers to human-made capital such as tools and machinery, but not to natural capital such as rivers and timber.

_____5.   If a production function exhibits constant returns to scale, then doubling all the inputs doubles the output.

_____6.   In very poor countries, paying parents to send their children to school could have a big impact on productivity.

_____7.   An increase in capital in a poor country should cause the country's growth rate to increase more than if the same increase in capital occurred in a rich country.

_____8.   An increase in the rate of saving and investment permanently increases a country's rate of growth.

_____9.   A country can increase its level of investment only by increasing its saving.

_____10.   The only factor of production that is not "produced" is natural resources.

_____11.   Investment in human capital may be particularly productive because of spillover effects, or externalities.

_____12.   In poorer countries, better nutrition leads to increases in the average height of the population and to higher productivity.

_____13.   Most economists believe that inward-oriented policies that protect infant industries improve the growth rates of developing nations.

_____14.   The opportunity cost of additional growth is that someone must forego current consumption.

_____15.   Some economists believe that world population growth has been an engine of technological progress and economic prosperity.

B. Multiple-Choice Questions

1.   Which one of the following is a reasonable measure of a country's standard of living?
   a.   real GDP per person
   b.   real GDP
   c.   nominal GDP per person
   d.   nominal GDP

2.   Which one of the following is the reason that South Korea has experienced more rapid economic growth than Canada?
   a.   South Korea has enormous natural resources.
   b.   South Korea started off poor, and it is now experiencing the "catch-up effect."
   c.   South Korea is an imperialist country that has collected wealth from previous victories in war.
   d.   South Korea has always been wealthy and will continue to be wealthy, which is known as the "snowball effect."

3.   Which one of the following statements is most likely when a nation has very little real GDP per person?
   a.   It must be a small nation.
   b.   It is doomed to being relatively poor forever.
   c.   An increase in capital will likely have little impact on output.
   d.   Inadequate nutrition is an obstacle to higher productivity.

4. Which one of the following statements is most likely once a country is wealthy?
    a. It no longer needs human capital.
    b. It is nearly impossible for it to become relatively poorer.
    c. Capital becomes more productive due to the "catch-up effect."
    d. It may be harder for it to grow quickly because of the diminishing returns to capital.

5. Which one of the following is the number of years it will take for nominal income to double if, using the rule of 70, the nominal income grows at 10 percent per year?
    a. approximately 7 years
    b. approximately 10 years
    c. approximately 70 years
    d. approximately 700 years

6. When Carly was born, her parents deposited $5000 in a bank account for her. Using the rule of 70, which one of the following is the amount that will be in the bank account when Carly retires at 70 years old, if the deposit earns 5 percent per year?
    a. $40 000
    b. $80 000
    c. $160 000
    d. $180 000

7. Two countries start with the same real GDP per person. One country grows at 2 percent, while the other grows at 4 percent. Which one of the following statements is most accurate?
    a. One country will always have 2 percent more real GDP per person than the other.
    b. The standard of living in the country growing at 4 percent will start to accelerate away from the slower growing country due to compound growth.
    c. The standard of living in the two countries will converge due to diminishing returns to capital.
    d. Next year, the country growing at 4 percent will be twice as large as the one growing at 2 percent.

8. Which one of the following is the opportunity cost of additional growth?
    a. a reduction in taxes
    b. a reduction in current saving
    c. a reduction in current investment
    d. a reduction in current consumption

9. Which one of the following is **NOT** associated with an expected increase in productivity within a nation?
    a. an increase in labour
    b. an increase in human capital per worker
    c. an increase in physical capital per worker
    d. an increase in natural resources per worker

10. Which one of the following statements is true? ·
    a. The level of GDP per person may be different for each country, but all countries grow at the same rate.
    b. The growth rate of each country may be different, but all countries have the same level of GDP per person.
    c. The level and growth rate of GDP per person varies by country; thus, a poor country can become relatively rich over time.
    d. All countries have the same growth rate and level of output because any country can obtain the same factors of production

11. If a production function exhibits constant returns to scale, which one of the following occurs if the inputs are doubled?
    a. Output doubles.
    b. Output more than doubles due to the catch-up effect.
    c. Output is less than double due to diminishing returns.
    d. Output is not impacted because output is constant.

12. Which one of the following is copper an example of?
    a. human capital
    b. physical capital
    c. a renewable natural resource
    d. a nonrenewable natural resource

13. Which one of the following describes an increase in technological knowledge?
    a. A farmer buys another tractor.
    b. A farmer hires another day labourer.
    c. A farmer discovers that it is better to plant in the spring than in the fall.
    d. A farmer sends his child to agricultural college and the child returns to work on the farm.

14. Which one of the following is a country's standard of living **MOST** closely related to?
    a. The country's supply of labour, because that determines how hard the citizens work.
    b. The country's supply of capital, because everything of value is produced by machinery.
    c. The country's supply of natural resources, because they limit production.
    d. The country's productivity, because income is equal to what is produced.

15.   Which one of the following is an example of foreign portfolio investment?
a. Honda builds a new plant in Ontario.
b. Royal Bank builds a new corporate office building.
c. A U.S. pension fund buys stock in Air Canada, and Air Canada uses the proceeds to buy new airplanes.
d. A Canadian citizen buys stock in Air Canada, and Air Canada uses the proceeds to buy a new airplane.

16.   Which one of the following government policies is likely to increase growth in Africa?
a. restrictions on foreign capital investment
b. increased spending on health and nutrition
c. decreased expenditures on public education
d. restrictions on property rights

17.   Which one of the following will occur if Toyota builds a new manufacturing plant in Ontario?
a. Canadian GDP will rise more than Canadian GNP.
b. Foreign portfolio investment in Canada will rise.
c. Canadian GDP will rise, but the increase will be less than that of Canadian GNP.
d. Canadian GDP and GNP will both fall because some income from this investment will accrue to foreigners.

18.   A country's real GDP per person in 2012 was $34 100, and real GDP per person in 2013 was $35 669. Which one of the following is the growth rate of real output per person over this period?
a. 2.6 percent
b. 3.6 percent
c. 4.6 percent
d. 5.6 percent

19.   Which one of the following expenditures to enhance productivity will emit a positive externality?
a. TD Canada Trust buys a new computer.
b. Susan pays her university tuition.
c. Imperial Oil explores a new oil field.
d. General Motors buys a new drill press.

20.   Which one of the following government policies will increase economic growth?
a. reduce property rights
b. encourage consumption
c. encourage research and development
d. restrict foreign investment

C. Short-Answer Questions

1. Economists measure both the level of real GDP per person and the growth rate of real GDP per person. Each statistic captures a different concept. Describe each concept. _____

    _____

2. What role does the World Bank play in economic growth? _____

    _____

    _____

    _____

3. In Canada, real GDP per person has grown at 2 percent per year. At this rate of growth, how long will it take for real GDP per person to double?

    _____

4. Which factors determine productivity? Which ones are human produced?

    _____

    _____

5. How does human capital differ from physical capital? _____

    _____

    _____

6. Explain the opportunity cost of investing in capital. Does any difference exist in the opportunity cost of investing in human capital versus physical capital?

    _____

    _____

    _____

7. Why does an increase in the rate of saving and investment only temporarily increase the rate of growth? _____

    _____

8. Foreigners buy newly issued stock in Air Canada, and then Air Canada uses the proceeds to expand capacity by buying new planes. Which will rise more, GDP or GNP? Why? What is this type of investment called? _____

    _____

    _____

    _____

    _____

9. How are property rights related to political stability? _____

    _____

    _____

    _____

10. How does population growth affect productivity? _____

_____

_____

_____

_____

D. Practice Problems

Use this table for questions 1 and 2.

Country	Current real GDP/person	Current growth rate
Northcountry	$15 468	1.98%
Southcountry	$13 690	2.03%
Eastcountry	$6 343	3.12%
Westcountry	$1 098	0.61%

1. a. Which country is richest? Explain. _____

_____

   b. Which country is advancing **MOST** quickly? Explain why. _____

_____

   c. Which country would likely see the greatest benefit from an increase in capital investment? Why? _____

_____

_____

   d. Refer to (c): Would this country continue to see the same degree of benefits from an increase in capital investment forever? Why or why not?

_____

_____

   e. Refer to (d): Why might investment in human capital and in research and development fail to exhibit the same degree of diminishing returns as investment in physical capital? _____

_____

_____

   f. Which country has the potential to grow **MOST** quickly? List some reasons why it may not be living up to potential. _____

_____

_____

_____

   g. If real GDP per person in Northcountry is $15 918 in the next year, what is its annual growth rate? _____

2. Suppose the real GDP per person in Fastcountry grows at an annual rate of 2 percent, and the real GDP per person in Slowcountry grows at an annual rate of 1 percent. Use the rule of 70 to answer the following questions. (Note: The rule of 70 is carefully explained in Helpful Hint #2 at the beginning of Chapter 7 in this *Study Guide*.)

   a. How many years does it take for real GDP per person to double in Fastcountry? _____

   _____

   b. If real GDP per person in Fastcountry is $2000 in 1930, how much will it be in the year 2000? _____

   _____

   c. How many years does it take for real GDP per person to double in Slowcountry? _____

   _____

   d. If real GDP per person in Slowcountry is $2000 in 1930, how much will it be in the year 2000? _____

   _____

   e. Using the above answers, explain the concept of compound growth.

   _____

   _____

   _____

   f. If Fastcountry stopped growing in the year 2000, how many years would it take for the standard of living in Slowcountry to catch up to that of Fastcountry? _____

   _____

3. Imagine a kitchen. It contains a cook, the cook's diploma, a recipe book, a stove and utensils, and some venison harvested from the open range.

   a. Link each object in the kitchen to a general category within the factors of production. _____

   _____

   _____

   _____

   b. While the different factors of production exhibit different levels of durability, which one is special in that it does not wear out? _____

   _____

   _____

E. Advanced Critical Thinking

The conversation of some students in their 20s turns to a supposed lack of growth and opportunity in Canada compared to some Asian countries such as South Korea and Singapore. One student says, "These Asian countries must have cheated somehow. That's the only way they could possibly have grown so quickly."

1. Have you learned anything in this chapter that would make you question this student's assertion? Explain. _____

   _____

   _____

2. The phenomenal growth rate of Japan since World War II has often been referred to as the "Japanese miracle." Is it a miracle or is it explainable? Clarify your answer. _____

   _____

   _____

3. Are the high growth rates found in these Asian countries without cost?

   _____

   _____

III. Solutions

A. True/False Questions

1. F; growth depends on the rate of increase in productivity.
2. T
3. F; the prices of most natural resources adjusted for inflation are stable or falling, reflecting our ability to conserve natural resources.
4. F; human capital is the knowledge and skills of workers.
5. T
6. T
7. T
8. F; due to diminishing returns to capital, growth rises temporarily.
9. F; it can attract foreign investment.
10. T
11. T
12. T
13. F; most economists believe that outward-oriented policies improve growth.
14. T.
15. T

B. Multiple-Choice Questions

1. a	5. a	9. a	13. c	17. a
2. b	6. c	10. c	14. d	18. c
3. d	7. b	11. a	15. c	19. b
4. d	8. d	12. d	16. b	20. c

C. Short-Answer Questions

1. Level of real GDP per person measures standard of living. Growth rate of real GDP per person measures rate of advance of the standard of living.

2. The World Bank obtains funds from the world's advanced countries and makes loans to less-developed countries so that they can invest in physical capital, such as roads and schools.

3. $70/2 = 35$ years

4. Physical capital per worker, human capital per worker, natural resources per worker, and technological knowledge. All except natural resources.

5. Human capital is the knowledge and skills of the worker. Physical capital is the stock of equipment and structures.

6. Someone must forgo current consumption. No; someone must save instead of consume, regardless of whether education or machines are purchased with the savings.

7. There are diminishing returns to physical capital.

8. GDP. GNP measures only the income of Canadians, while GDP measures income generated inside Canada. Therefore, GDP will rise more than GNP because some of the profits from the capital investment will accrue to foreigners in the form of dividends. This type of investment is called foreign portfolio investment.

9. Countries with a poor court system, corrupt officials, and frequent revolutions are much less likely to respect property rights.

10. On the one hand, when population growth is rapid, each worker is equipped with less capital, which leads to lower productivity. On the other hand, if the population is larger, then more scientists and inventors will exist to contribute to technological advancements, which lead to higher productivity.

D. Practice Problems

1. a. Northcountry, because it has the largest real GDP per person

    b. Eastcountry, because it has the largest growth rate

    c. Westcountry is the poorest and likely has the least capital. Because capital exhibits diminishing returns, it is most productive when it is relatively scarce.

    d. No, because of diminishing returns to capital, the additional growth from increasing capital declines as a country has more capital.

    e. Human capital emits a positive externality. Research and development is a public good after dissemination.

    f. Westcountry, because it is currently the poorest and could easily benefit from additional capital. It may have trade restrictions (inward-oriented policies), a corrupt or unstable government, few courts, a lack of established property rights, poor health and nutrition, etc.

    g. ($15 918 – $15 468)/$15 468 = 0.029 = 2.9%

2. a. 70/2 = 35 years

    b. $8000

    c. 70/1 = 70 years

    d. $4000

    e. Fastcountry adds $2000 to its GDP in the first 35 years. Growing at the same 2 percent rate, it adds $4000 to its GDP over the next 35 years because the same growth rate is now applied to a larger base.

    f. another 70 years

3. a. Cook = labour, diploma = human capital, recipe book = technological knowledge, stove and utensils = physical capital, venison = natural resource.

    b. Recipes (technological knowledge) never wear out. Labour and human capital depreciate, the stove and utensils wear out slowly, and the venison is used up (although probably renewable).

E. Advanced Critical Thinking

1. Yes. There are many sources of growth and a country can influence all of them except natural resources.

2. Japan's growth is explainable. Indeed, all the high-growth Asian countries have extremely high investment as a percent of GDP.

3. No. The opportunity cost of investment is that someone must forgo current consumption in order to save and invest.

8 Saving, Investment, and the Financial System

I. Chapter Overview

A. Context and Purpose

Chapter 8 is the second chapter in a three-chapter sequence about the production of output in the long run. Chapter 7 explained that capital and labour are among the primary determinants of output in the long run. For this reason, Chapter 8 addresses the financial system and the market for saving and investment in capital, while Chapter 9 will address the market for labour.

The purpose of Chapter 8 is to show how saving and investment are coordinated by the loanable funds market. Within the framework of the loanable funds market, we are able to see the effects of taxes and of government budget deficits and surpluses on saving, investment, the accumulation of capital, and, ultimately, the growth rate of output.

B. Helpful Hints

1. *A financial intermediary is a middleman.* An intermediary is someone who gets between two groups and negotiates a solution. For example, intermediaries in labour negotiations sit between a firm and a union. In a like manner, a bank is a financial intermediary in that it sits between the ultimate lender (the depositor) and the ultimate borrower (the firm or home builder) and "negotiates" the terms of the loan contracts. Banks do not lend their own money. They lend the depositor's money.

2. *Investment is not the purchase of stocks and bonds.* In casual conversation, people use the word "investment" to mean the purchase of stocks and bonds. For example, "I just invested in ten shares of Bell Canada." (Even an economist might say this.) However, when speaking in economic terms, *investment* is the actual purchase of capital structures and equipment. In this technical framework, when a person buys ten shares of newly issued Bell Canada stock, there has been only an exchange of assets—Bell Canada has the buyer's money and the buyer has the stock certificates. If Bell Canada uses the money to buy new equipment, the purchase of the equipment is economic *investment*.

3. *Do not include consumption loans in the supply of loanable funds.* In casual conversation, people use the word "saving" to refer to their new bank deposits. For example, "I just saved $100 this week." (An economist might say this, too.) However, if that deposit were loaned out to a consumer who used the funds to purchase airline tickets for a vacation, there has been no increase in *national*

saving (or just *saving*) in a macroeconomic sense. This is because saving, in a macroeconomic sense, is income (GDP) that remains after *national* consumption expenditures and government purchases ($S = Y - C - G$). No national saving took place if a personal saving was loaned and used for consumption expenditures by another person. Because national saving is the source of the supply of loanable funds, consumption loans do not affect the supply of loanable funds.

4. *Demand for loanable funds is private demand for investment funds.* The demand for loanable funds includes only private (households and firms) demand for funds to invest in capital structures and equipment. When government runs a deficit, it does absorb national saving but it does not buy capital equipment with the funds. Therefore, when government runs a deficit, it is considered a reduction in the supply of loanable funds, not an increase in the demand for loanable funds.

II. Self-Testing Challenges

A. True/False Questions

_____1.   When a business firm sells a bond, it has engaged in equity finance.

_____2.   People who buy stock in a firm have loaned money to the firm.

_____3.   The credit risk of a bond is the probability that the borrower will fail to pay some of the interest or principal.

_____4.   Federal government bonds pay less interest than corporate bonds because the federal government is a safer credit risk.

_____5.   In a closed economy, saving is what remains after consumption expenditures and government purchases.

_____6.   Public saving is always positive.

_____7.   In a closed economy, investment is always equal to saving regardless of where the saving came from—i.e., whether the source was public or private.

_____8.   The GST is a consumption tax that encourages greater saving.

_____9.   If Andy saves money this week and subsequently lends it to his roommate to buy food for consumption, Andy's act of personal saving has increased national saving.

_____10.   The quantity of loanable funds supplied is greater if real interest rates are higher.

_____11.   If the real interest rate in the loanable funds market is temporarily held above the equilibrium rate, desired borrowing will exceed desired lending, and the real interest rate will fall.

_____12.   Net debt is the difference between the value of government financial assets and the value of government financial liabilities.

_____13.   Public saving and the government budget surplus are the same thing.

_____14.   If the government wants to increase the rate of growth, it should raise taxes on interest and dividends to shift the supply of loanable funds to the right.

_____15.   Some economists believe that unfunded financial liabilities should also be included in the government debt estimates.

B. Multiple-Choice Questions

1.   Which one of the following is an example of equity finance?
   a.   stock
   b.   bank loan
   c.   corporate bonds
   d.   provincial government bonds

2.   Which one of the following defines a bond's credit risk?
   a.   a bond's term to maturity
   b.   a bond's probability of default
   c.   a bond's tax treatment
   d.   a bond's dividend

3.   Which one of the following is an example of a financial intermediary?
   a.   a middleman between labour unions and firms
   b.   a middleman between husbands and wives
   c.   a middleman between buyers and sellers
   d.   a middleman between borrowers and lenders

4.   Which one of the following is equal to national saving (or just saving)?
   a.   private saving + public saving
   b.   investment + consumption expenditures
   c.   GDP – government purchases
   d.   GDP – consumption expenditures

5.   Which one of the following statements is true?
   a.   A stock index is a directory used to locate information about selected stocks.
   b.   Longer term bonds tend to pay less interest than shorter term bonds.
   c.   Federal government bonds tend to pay less interest than corporate bonds.
   d.   Professional money managers consistently "beat the market."

6.   Which one of the following occurs if government spending exceeds tax collections?
   a.   There is a budget surplus.
   b.   There is a budget deficit.
   c.   Private saving is negative.
   d.   Public saving is positive.

7.   If GDP = $1000, consumption = $600, taxes = $100, and government purchases = $200, which choice below indicates how much saving and investment are?
   a.   saving = $200; investment = $200
   b.   saving = $300; investment = $300
   c.   saving = $100; investment = $200
   d.   saving = $200; investment = $100

8.   Which one of the following statements describes the outcome if the public consumes $10 billion less and the government purchases $10 billion more (assuming other things are unchanged)?
   a.   Saving remains the same.
   b.   There is a decrease in saving and the economy should grow more slowly.
   c.   There is an increase in saving and the economy should grow more quickly.

9.   Which one of the following financial market securities would likely pay the highest interest rate?
   a.   a federal government bond
   b.   a bond issued by Bell Canada
   c.   a bond issued by a start-up company
   d.   a government bond issued by the province of Ontario

10.   Which one of the following is synonymous with investment?
   a.   the purchase of shares in a mutual fund
   b.   the purchase of goods and services
   c.   the placement of savings in a bank account
   d.   the purchase of capital equipment and structures

11.   Which one of the following would be expected to occur if Canadians saved a greater percentage of their income?
   a.   The supply of loanable funds would shift to the right and the real interest rate would rise.
   b.   The supply of loanable funds would shift to the right and the real interest rate would fall.
   c.   The demand for loanable funds would shift to the right and the real interest rate would rise.
   d.   The demand for loanable funds would shift to the right and the real interest rate would fall.

12.   Which one of the following sets of government policies is the **MOST** growth oriented?
   a.   lower taxes on the returns to saving, provide investment tax credits, and lower the deficit
   b.   lower taxes on the returns to saving, provide investment tax credits, and increase the deficit
   c.   increase taxes on the returns to saving, provide investment tax credits, and lower the deficit
   d.   increase taxes on the returns to saving, provide investment tax credits, and increase the deficit

13.   Which one of the following occurs when an increase in a budget deficit causes a government to increase its borrowing?
   a.   Demand for loanable funds shifts to the right.
   b.   Demand for loanable funds shifts to the left.
   c.   Supply of loanable funds shifts to the left.
   d.   Supply of loanable funds shifts to the right.

14.   Which one of the following describes the outcomes of an increase in budget deficit?
   a.   The real interest rate will be higher and the quantity of loanable funds demanded for investment will be decreased.
   b.   The real interest rate will be higher and the quantity of loanable funds demanded for investment will be increased.
   c.   The real interest rate will be lower and the quantity of loanable funds demanded for investment will be increased.
   d.   The real interest rate will be lower and the quantity of loanable funds demanded for investment will be decreased.

15.   If the supply of loanable funds is very inelastic (steep), which one of the following policies would likely increase saving and investment the **MOST**?
   a.   an investment tax credit
   b.   an increase in a budget surplus
   c.   an increase in a budget deficit
   d.   decreasing the GST consumption tax from 5 percent to 4 percent

16.   Which one of the following is synonymous with an increase in a budget surplus?
   a.   a decrease in public saving
   b.   an increase in public saving
   c.   a decrease in private saving
   d.   an increase in private saving

17.   Which one of the following terms describes a scenario in which a series of budget surpluses stimulates investment, thus resulting in faster economic growth and even higher budget surpluses?
    a.   equity finance
    b.   debt finance
    c.   virtuous circle
    d.   vicious circle

18.   If Canadians become less concerned with the future and save less at each real interest rate, which one of the following will occur?
    a.   Real interest rates will fall and investment will fall.
    b.   Real interest rates will fall and investment will rise.
    c.   Real interest rates will rise and investment will fall.
    d.   Real interest rates will rise and investment will rise.

C. Short-Answer Questions

1.   Explain why a mutual fund is likely to be a less risky purchase than an individual stock.

_____

_____

2.   Which is likely to give you a greater rate of return, a chequing deposit at a bank or the purchase of a corporate bond? Why? _____

_____

_____

_____

3.   What is the difference between debt finance and equity finance? Provide an example of each. _____

_____

_____

4.   What is meant by the words "saving" and "investment" in the national income accounts, and how do these meanings differ from the casual use of the words?

_____

_____

_____

_____

5.   In a closed economy, why can investment never exceed saving? _____

_____

_____

_____

6.   What is meant by a vicious circle? _____

_____

_____

_____

7.   Utilizing the national income identities, if government purchases were to rise, and if output, taxes, and consumption were to remain unchanged, what would happen to national saving, investment, and growth? _____

_____

_____

_____

_____

8.   Suppose Canadians consume a smaller percent of their income and save a larger percent. Describe the consequent changes in the loanable funds market. What would likely happen to growth? _____

_____

_____

_____

_____

9.   Suppose government runs a larger budget surplus. Describe the consequent changes in the loanable funds market. What would likely happen to growth?

_____

_____

_____

_____

10.   An increase in a government's budget deficit forces a government to borrow more. Why does an increase in a deficit fail to increase the demand for loanable funds in the loanable funds market? _____

_____

_____

_____

_____

11.   What is the difference between financial markets and financial intermediaries?

_____

_____

_____

_____

_____

D. Practice Problems

1. Fly-by-Night Corporation is in need of capital funds to expand its production capacity. It is selling short-term and long-term bonds and is issuing stock. Sven is considering the prospect of helping finance the expansion.

    a. If Sven is buying both short-term and long-term to maturity bonds from Fly-by-Night Corporation, from which bond would Sven demand a higher rate of return, the short-term bond or the long-term bond? Why?

    _____

    _____

    b. If the Dominion Bond Rating Service lowered the credit worthiness of Fly-by-Night Corporation, would this affect the rate of return Sven would demand when buying the bonds? Why or why not? _____

    _____

    c. If Fly-by-Night Corporation is issuing both stocks and bonds, from which would Sven expect to earn the higher rate of return over the long run? Why?

    _____

    _____

    d. Which would be safer: (1) Sven puts all his personal saving into Fly-by-Night Corporation stock, or (2) Sven puts all his personal saving into a mutual fund that has some Fly-by-Night Corporation stock in its portfolio? Why?

    _____

    _____

2. Use the saving and investment identities from the National Income Accounts to answer the following questions. Suppose the following values are from the national income accounts of a country with a closed economy. (All values are in billions.)

    $Y = \$600$
    $T = \$100$
    $C = \$400$
    $G = \$120$

    a. What is the value of saving and investment in this country? _____

    _____

    b. What is the value of private saving? _____

    _____

    c. What is the value of public saving? _____

    _____

d. Is government budget policy contributing to growth in this country or harming it? Why? _____

_____

_____

e. Why is it that countries find it difficult to reduce their budget deficits?

_____

3. The following information describes a loanable funds market. (Values are in billions.)

Real interest rate	Quantity of loanable funds supplied	Quantity of loanable funds demanded
6%	$130	$70
5%	$120	$80
4%	$100	$100
3%	$80	$120
2%	$60	$160

a. Plot the supply and demand for loanable funds. What are the equilibrium real interest rate and the equilibrium level of saving and investment?

_____

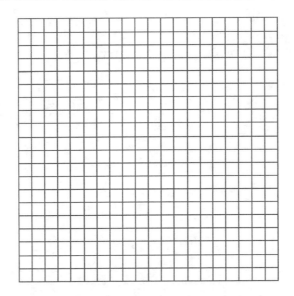

b. What "market forces" will not allow 2 percent to be the real interest rate?

_____

_____

_____

c. Suppose the government suddenly increases its budget deficit by $40 billion. What are the new equilibrium real interest rate and the equilibrium level of saving and investment? Explain and show graphically. _____

_____

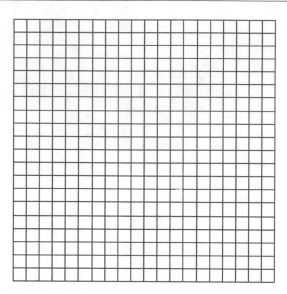

d. Starting at the original equilibrium, suppose the government enacts an investment tax credit that stimulates the demand for loanable funds for capital investment by $40 billion at any real interest rate. What are the new equilibrium real interest rate and the equilibrium level of saving and investment? Explain and show graphically. _____

_____

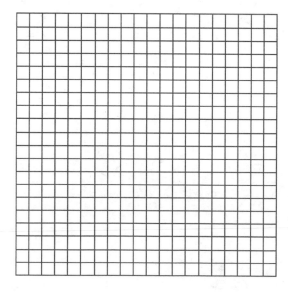

e. With respect to (c) and (d), which policy is **MOST** likely to increase growth? Why? _____

_____

_____

_____

E. Advanced Critical Thinking

During a political debate, a candidate is questioned about her position on economic growth. She says, "We need to get this country growing again. We need to use tax cuts to stimulate saving and investment, and we need to get that budget deficit down so that the government stops absorbing our nation's saving."

1. If government spending remains unchanged, what inconsistency is implied by the candidate's statement? _____

_____

_____

2. If the candidate truly wishes to decrease taxes and decrease the budget deficit, what has she implied about her plans for government spending? _____

_____

_____

3. If policymakers want to increase growth, and if policymakers have to choose between tax incentives to stimulate saving and tax incentives to stimulate investment, what might they want to know about supply and demand in the loanable funds market before making their decision? Explain. _____

_____

_____

_____

_____

_____

_____

_____

III. Solutions

A. True/False Questions

1. F; to sell a bond is to engage in debt finance.
2. F; shareholders are owners.
3. T
4. T
5. T
6. F; public saving is negative when a government budget deficit exists.
7. T
8. T
9. F; consumption loans do not increase national saving.
10. T
11. F; desired lending exceeds desired borrowing.
12. T
13. T
14. F; it should lower taxes on interest and dividends.
15. T

B. Multiple-Choice Questions

1. a	5. c	9. c	13. c	17. c
2. b	6. b	10. d	14. a	18. c
3. d	7. a	11. b	15. b	
4. a	8. a	12. a	16. b	

C. Short-Answer Questions

1. A mutual fund is diversified. When one stock in the fund is performing poorly, it is likely that another stock is performing well.

2. A corporate bond will likely give a greater rate of return because the bond is riskier, and because "direct" lending through a financial market has fewer overhead costs than "indirect" lending through an intermediary.

3. Debt finance is borrowing, such as when a firm sells a bond. Equity finance is taking on additional owners of the firm, such as when a firm sells stock.

4. Saving is what remains after consumption and government purchases. Investment is the purchase of equipment and structures. In casual conversation, saving is what remains of a person's income after consumption, and investment is the purchase of stocks and bonds.

5. Investment never exceed saving in a closed economy because saving is the GDP left over after consumption expenditures and government purchases, and this is the limit of the income available for purchasing equipment and structures.

6. A vicious circle happens when budget deficits increase interest rates, discourage investment, and slow economic growth. The slower growth leads to lower tax revenues, resulting in even higher budget deficits.

7. Public saving would decrease and cause national saving and investment to decrease by the same amount, slowing growth.

8. The supply of loanable funds would shift right, the real interest rate would fall, and the quantity of loanable funds demanded to purchase capital would increase. Growth would increase.

9. The supply of loanable funds would shift right, the real interest rate would fall, and the quantity of loanable funds demanded to purchase capital would increase. Growth would increase.

10. The demand for loanable funds is defined as *private* demand for borrowing to purchase capital equipment and structures. An increase in a deficit absorbs saving and reduces the supply of loanable funds.

11. In a financial market, savers lend directly to borrowers. Through financial intermediaries, savers lend to an intermediary who then lends to the borrower.

D. Practice Problems

1. a. Long-term, because it is more likely that Sven may need to sell the long-term bond before maturity at a depressed price.

    b. Yes; the credit risk has increased and lenders would demand a higher rate of return.

    c. Owners of stock demand a higher rate of return because stocks are riskier.

    d. It is safer to put money in a mutual fund because it is diversified (i.e., not all one's eggs are in one basket).

2. a. ($600 − $100 − $400) + ($100 − $120) = $80 billion

    b. $600 − $100 − $400 = $100 billion

    c. $100 − $120 = −$20 billion

d. It is harming growth because public saving is negative, and therefore less national saving is available for investment.

e. Politicians find it politically difficult to increase taxes or decrease spending.

3. a. Equilibrium real interest rate = 4%. Equilibrium S and I = $100 billion.

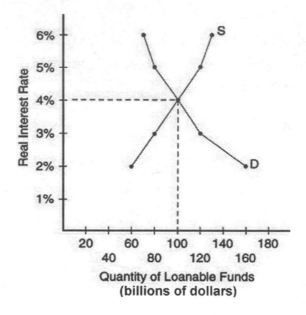

b. At 2 percent interest, the quantity demanded of loanable funds exceeds the quantity supplied by $100 billion. This excess demand for loans (borrowing) will drive interest rates up to 4 percent.

c. Equilibrium real interest rate = 5%. Equilibrium S and I = $80 billion.

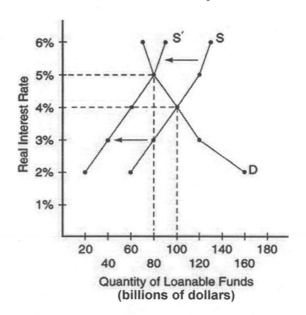

d. Equilibrium real interest rate = 5%. Equilibrium *S* and *I* = $120 billion.

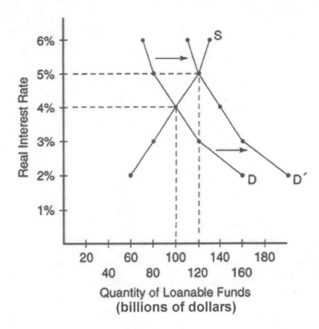

e. An investment tax credit; it shifts the demand for loanable funds to invest in capital to the right, thus raising the level of investment in capital and stimulating growth.

E. Advanced Critical Thinking

1. Tax cuts to stimulate saving and investment would increase the deficit, which would reduce national saving and investment.

2. The candidate plans to reduce government spending by even more than she cuts taxes.

3. Policymakers would want to know the elasticity of the supply and demand curves. If loanable funds demand is inelastic, changes in loanable funds supply have little effect on saving and investment, and therefore tax incentives to increase saving at each interest rate do little for growth. If loanable funds supply is inelastic, changes in loanable funds demand have little effect on saving and investment, and therefore tax incentives to increase investment at each interest rate do little for growth.

CHAPTER 9 Unemployment and Its Natural Rate

I. Chapter Overview

A. Context and Purpose

Chapter 9 is the third chapter in a three-chapter sequence on the level and growth of output in the long run. In Chapter 7, we learned that capital and labour are among the primary determinants of output and growth. In Chapter 8, we addressed how saving and investment in capital goods affect the production of output. Here in Chapter 9, we see how full utilization of our labour resources improves the level of production and our standard of living.

The purpose of Chapter 9 is to introduce the labour market. It explains how economists measure the performance of the labour market using unemployment statistics. Chapter 9 also examines the four factors that cause unemployment in the long run, and the effects of government policies on the natural rate of unemployment.

B. Helpful Hints

1. *Job search takes time even at the competitive equilibrium wage.* Minimum-wage laws, unions, and efficiency wages all create an excess supply of labour, called structural unemployment, by holding the wage above the competitive equilibrium wage. However, the frictional unemployment that arises from the process of job search occurs at the competitive equilibrium wage because it is inevitable that it takes time for workers and firms to match, regardless of the wage.

2. *The natural rate of unemployment is persistent, not constant.* Minimum-wage laws, unions, efficiency wages, and job search all have impacts on the natural rate of unemployment. Therefore, the natural rate of unemployment will change as government policies, institutions, and behaviours change. But because policies, institutions, and behaviours change slowly, so does the natural rate of unemployment. Note then, that the natural rate of unemployment is estimated to have been as low as 4 percent in the late 1960s, and as high as 8 percent in the late 1980s.

II. Self-Testing Challenges

A. True/False Questions

_____1.   The natural rate of unemployment is the amount of unemployment that will not go away on its own, even in the long run.

_____2.   If the unemployment rate falls, it is certain that more workers have jobs.

_____3.   In post-World War II Canada, the labour-force participation rate has been rising for women and has been falling for men.

_____4.   The unemployment rate is the percentage of the adult population that is unemployed.

_____5.   A minimum wage is likely to have a greater impact on the market for skilled workers than on the market for unskilled workers.

_____6.   The presence of a union tends to raise the wage for insiders and lower the wage for outsiders.

_____7.   Three-fifths of unemployed Canadians are unemployed for more than three months.

_____8.   The 2008–2009 recession raised the unemployment rate of females more than the unemployment rate of males.

_____9.   An efficiency wage is like a minimum wage in that firms are required by legislation to pay it.

_____10.   Paying efficiency wages tends to increase worker turnover because workers can get continually higher wages if they "job hop."

_____11.   If a firm pays above the competitive equilibrium wage, its worker pool may increase because better quality candidates tend to apply for the firm's job openings.

_____12.   If wages were always at the competitive equilibrium, there would be absolutely no unemployment.

_____13.   If there are "discouraged searchers," the measured unemployment rate overstates true unemployment.

_____14.   Sectoral shifts refer to changes in the composition of demand among industries or regions of the country.

____15.   Changes to Canada's Employment Insurance program in the 1990s lowered Canada's natural unemployment rate.

B. Multiple-Choice Questions

1.   Which one of the following refers to the amount of unemployment that the economy normally experiences?
   a.   union unemployment
   b.   cyclical unemployment
   c.   efficiency wage unemployment
   d.   natural rate of unemployment

2.   According to Statistics Canada, which one of the following refers to a husband who chooses to stay home and take care of the household?
   a.   employed
   b.   unemployed
   c.   not in the labour force
   d.   a discouraged searcher

Use the following table for questions 3–5.

	Quantity (millions)
Total population	29.7
Adult population	21.2
Unemployed	1.2
Employed	12.1

3.   Which one of the following is the size of the labour force?
   a.   12.1 million
   b.   13.3 million
   c.   20.0 million
   d.   21.2 million

4.   Which one of the following is the unemployment rate?
   a.   5.7 percent
   b.   6.0 percent
   c.   9.0 percent
   d.   9.9 percent

5.   Which one of the following is the labour-force participation rate?
   a.   40.7 percent
   b.   44.8 percent
   c.   57.1 percent
   d.   62.7 percent

6. Which one of the following refers to an accountant with a CA designation who has been unable to find work for so long that she has stopped looking for work?
   a. She is considered to be employed.
   b. She is considered to be unemployed.
   c. She is not considered to be in the labour force.
   d. She is not considered to be in the adult population.

7. Which one of the following statements is true?
   a. The labour-force participation rate of men is rising.
   b. Women tend to have a higher labour-force participation rate than men.
   c. Younger workers tend to have lower unemployment rates than older workers.
   d. Generally, similarly aged men and women tend to have similar rates of unemployment.

8. Which one of the following tends to be an effect of the minimum-wage law?
   a. It creates more unemployment in high-skill job markets than in low-skill job markets.
   b. It creates more unemployment in low-skill job markets than in high-skill job markets.
   c. It has no impact on unemployment as long as it is set above the competitive equilibrium wage.
   d. It helps all teenagers because they receive a higher wage than they would otherwise.

9. Which of the following sources of unemployment is **NOT** based on the wage being held above the competitive equilibrium wage?
   a. unemployment due to unions
   b. unemployment due to job search
   c. unemployment due to efficiency wages
   d. unemployment due to minimum-wage laws

10. Which one of the following will result if, for any reason, the wage is held above the competitive equilibrium wage?
    a. Unions will likely strike, and the wage will fall to equilibrium.
    b. The quality of workers will fall due to the change in the number of workers in the applicant pool.
    c. The quantity of labour demanded will exceed the quantity of labour supplied, and there will be a labour shortage.
    d. The quantity of labour supplied will exceed the quantity of labour demanded, and there will be structural unemployment.

11. Which one of the following defines efficiency wage?
    a. the competitive equilibrium wage
    b. the above-equilibrium wage paid by firms
    c. the minimum wage the firm is willing to pay
    d. the minimum wage the worker is willing to accept

12. Which one of the following government policies would increase the unemployment rate?
    a. raising the minimum wage
    b. establishing employment agencies
    c. establishing worker training programs
    d. reducing Employment Insurance benefits

13. Which one of the following types of unemployment tends to be raised by sectoral shifts?
    a. frictional unemployment
    b. structural unemployment
    c. cyclical unemployment
    d. seasonal unemployment

14. Which one of the following is **NOT** a reason why firms may want to pay high wages?
    a. improved worker health
    b. increased worker turnover
    c. increased worker effort
    d. improved worker quality

15. Which one of the following countries has the **LOWEST** rate of union membership?
    a. Canada
    b. Sweden
    c. Denmark
    d. United States

16. Which one of the following describes how unions might increase efficiency?
    a. by lowering the wage of local outsiders
    b. by offsetting the market power of a large firm in a company town
    c. by raising the wage for insiders above the competitive equilibrium
    d. by threatening a strike but not actually following through, and therefore no hours of work are lost

17. Which one of the following statements about efficiency wage theory is true?
    a. Paying the lowest possible wage is always the most efficient (profitable).
    b. Paying above the competitive equilibrium wage causes workers to shirk their responsibilities.
    c. Firms do not have a choice about whether they pay efficiency wages or not because these wages are determined by law.
    d. Paying above the competitive equilibrium wage may improve worker health, lower worker turnover, improve worker quality, and increase worker effort.

18. Which one of the following describes how unions tend to increase the disparity in pay between insiders and outsiders?
    a. by increasing the demand for workers in the unionized sector
    b. by decreasing the supply of workers in the unionized sector
    c. by increasing the wage in the unionized sector, which may create an increase in the supply of workers in the nonunionized sector
    d. by increasing the wage in the unionized sector, which may create a decrease in the supply of workers in the nonunionized sector

19. Which one of the following types of unemployment will exist even if wages are at the competitive equilibrium?
    a. unemployment due to unions
    b. unemployment due to job search
    c. unemployment due to efficiency wages
    d. unemployment due to minimum-wage laws

20. Which one of the following would occur if Employment Insurance benefits were so generous that laid-off workers would be paid 95 percent of their regular salary?
    a. Frictional unemployment would fall.
    b. There would be no impact on measured unemployment.
    c. Measured unemployment would probably understate true unemployment.
    d. Measured unemployment would probably overstate true unemployment.

C. Short-Answer Questions

1. Give two reasons why the unemployment rate is an imperfect measure of joblessness. _____
   _____
   _____
   _____

2. In which of these two situations would a labour union be more likely to increase efficiency rather than reduce it: in a small, remote town with one large employer; or in a major city with many employers? Why? _____
   _____
   _____
   _____

3. Describe two ways that a union increases the disparity in the wages of members and nonmembers. _____
   _____
   _____
   _____
   _____

4. Does the minimum wage cause much unemployment in the market for accountants? Why or why not? _____

_____

_____

_____

5. Which type of unemployment will occur even if the wage is at the competitive equilibrium? Why? _____

_____

_____

_____

6. How does Employment Insurance increase frictional unemployment?

_____

_____

_____

_____

7. How might the government help reduce frictional unemployment?

_____

_____

_____

_____

8. Which of the following individuals is **MOST** likely to be unemployed for the long term: a fisherman who loses his job when the fish stocks decline, or a waitress who is laid off when a new cafe opens in town? Why?

_____

_____

_____

_____

9. Why do firms care about reducing worker turnover? _____

_____

_____

_____

_____

10. How does the "living wage" differ from the minimum wage? _____

_____

_____

_____

_____

D. Practice Problems

1. Use the following information about Country A to answer all parts of this question.

	2012 (millions)	2013 (millions)
Population	223.6	226.5
Adult population	168.2	169.5
Unemployed	7.4	8.1
Employed	105.2	104.2

a. How many people were in the labour force in 2012? How many people were in the labour force in 2013? _____

_____

_____

_____

b. What was the labour-force participation rate in 2012? What was the labour-force participation rate in 2013? _____

_____

_____

_____

c. What was the unemployment rate in 2012? What was the unemployment rate in 2013? _____

_____

_____

_____

d. From 2012 to 2013, the adult population went up, while the labour force went down. Provide a number of explanations why this might have occurred.

_____

_____

_____

_____

_____

_____

e. If the natural rate of unemployment in Country A is 6.6 percent, how much is cyclical unemployment in 2012 and 2013? Is Country A likely to be experiencing a recession in either of these years? _____

_____

_____

_____

_____

2. Suppose the labour market is segmented into two distinct markets: the market for low-skill workers and the market for high-skill workers. Further, suppose the competitive equilibrium wage in the low-skill market is $5.00 per hour, while the competitive equilibrium wage in the high-skill market is $25.00 per hour.

a. If the minimum wage is set at $9.00 per hour, which market will exhibit the greatest amount of unemployment? Demonstrate it graphically.

_____

_____

b. Does the minimum wage have any impact on the high-skill market? Why or why not? _____

_____

c. Do your results seem consistent with labour market statistics? Explain.

_____

_____

d. Suppose the high-skill market becomes unionized and the new negotiated wage is $28.00 per hour. Will this have any effect on the low-skill market? Explain. _____

_____

_____

_____

3. Answer the following questions about the composition of unemployment.

    a. What are some sources of unemployment? _____

    _____

    _____

    b. Which source of unemployment is initiated by a firm? _____

    _____

    c. Why might a firm pay wages in excess of the competitive equilibrium?

    _____

    _____

    d. Which type of efficiency wage is unlikely to be relevant to Canada? Why?

    _____

    _____

    _____

    e. How does job search unemployment differ from the other sources of
        unemployment? _____

    _____

    _____

E. Advanced Critical Thinking

Two roommates, David and Leon, are watching the national news on television. The
news anchor says, "Unemployment statistics released by Statistics Canada today show
an increase in unemployment from 6.4 percent to 6.6 percent. This is the third month in
a row where the unemployment rate has increased." David says to Leon, "Lately, there
are fewer and fewer people with jobs. I do not know how long Canada can continue like
this."

1. Can David's statement be deduced from the unemployment rate statistic? Why or
    why not? _____

    _____

    _____

    _____

    _____

2. What information would David need to determine whether there are really fewer
    people with jobs? _____

    _____

    _____

III. Solutions

A. True/False Questions

1. T
2. F; the unemployment rate falls when unemployed workers leave the labour force.
3. T
4. F; the percentage of the labour force that is unemployed.
5. F; a minimum wage has a greater impact on low-wage workers.
6. T
7. F; three-fifths are unemployed for less than three months.
8. F; it affected the unemployment rate of males more than that of females.
9. F; efficiency wages are paid voluntarily by firms.
10. F; efficiency wages reduce turnover.
11. T
12. F; there would still be frictional unemployment due to job search.
13. F; the measured unemployment rate understates true unemployment.
14. T
15. T

B. Multiple-Choice Questions

1. d	5. d	9. b	13. a	17. d
2. c	6. c	10. d	14. b	18. c
3. b	7. d	11. b	15. d	19. b
4. c	8. b	12. a	16. b	20. d

C. Short-Answer Questions

1. Some people claim to be looking for work just to collect Employment Insurance benefits. Others are discouraged searchers and have stopped looking for work due to an unsuccessful search.

2. A labour union would be more likely to increase efficiency in a small "company" town where a single company has market power that may depress the wage below the competitive equilibrium. This may need to be offset by organized labour.

3. It raises the wage above the competitive equilibrium in the unionized sector. Some of those unemployed in the unionized sector move to the nonunionized sector, thus increasing the supply of labour and lowering the wage in the nonunionized sector.

4. No, minimum wage does not cause much unemployment in the market for accountants because the competitive equilibrium wage for accountants exceeds the minimum wage; hence, the minimum wage is not a binding constraint for accountants.

5. Frictional unemployment will still occur because job matching takes time even when the wage is at the competitive equilibrium. Also, continuous sectoral shifts and new entrants into the job market make some job search unemployment inevitable.

6. Unemployed workers might devote less effort to their job search, and possibly turn down unattractive job offers, and Employment Insurance benefits influence the decisions of some people to enter the labour force.

7. The government might help reduce frictional employment by establishing government-run employment agencies and worker training programs to retrain workers that are laid off in the contracting sectors for jobs in growing industries.

8. The fisherman is most likely to be unemployed. He will have to retrain because the contraction of the fish stocks is likely permanent, while the waitress may just have to relocate, possibly just down the street.

9. It is costly for firms to hire and train new workers, and new workers are likely to be less productive than experienced workers. Firms with higher turnover therefore have higher production costs.

10. The minimum wage applies to all employees in a province, while a living wage is defined by a municipal law that applies only to firms hoping to win contracts from a particular municipal government.

D. Practice Problems

1. a.   2012: $7.4 + 105.2 = 112.6$ million
        2013: $8.1 + 104.2 = 112.3$ million

    b.   2012: $(112.6/168.2) \times 100 = 66.9\%$
        2013: $(112.3/169.5) \times 100 = 66.3\%$

    c.   2012: $(7.4/112.6) \times 100 = 6.6\%$
        2013: $(8.1/112.3) \times 100 = 7.2\%$

    d.   Some explanations are: earlier retirements, students staying in university longer, more parents staying at home with children, discouraged searchers discontinuing their job search.

    e.   2012: $6.6\% - 6.6\% = 0\%$
        2013: $7.2\% - 6.6\% = 0.6\%$

        In 2012, unemployment is "normal" for Country A; therefore there is no recession. However, in 2013, unemployment is above normal (positive cyclical unemployment); therefore Country A may be in a recession.

2. a. The low-skill market will experience unemployment because an excess supply of labour will exist.

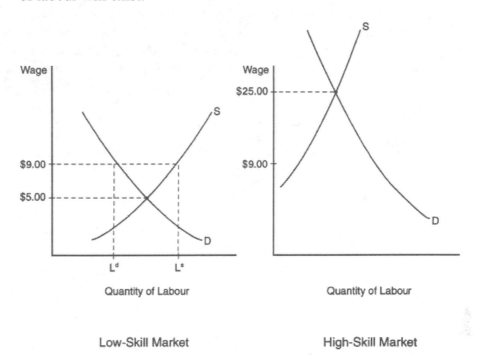

Low-Skill Market   High-Skill Market

b. No, because the competitive equilibrium wage is above the wage floor.

c. Yes. We observe a greater amount of unemployment among low-skill workers, who are often young and inexperienced.

d. Yes. The excess supply of skilled workers may cause some skilled workers to move to the unskilled market. This would increase the supply of labour in the unskilled market and cause even more unemployment in the unskilled market.

3. a. Some sources of unemployment are the minimum wage, unions, efficiency wages, and job search.

b. A source of unemployment initiated by a firm is efficiency wages.

c. A firm might pay wages in excess of the competitive equilibrium in order to improve worker health, lower worker turnover, increase worker effort, or improve worker quality.

d. The efficiency wage that is unlikely to be relevant to Canada is worker health because, in Canada, workers' wages are significantly above the level needed for an adequate diet.

e. Job search, or frictional, unemployment exists even when the wage is at a competitive equilibrium.

E. Advanced Critical Thinking

1. No. The unemployment rate is the *ratio* of the number of unemployed to the labour force. If the labour force grows (e.g., new graduates, homemakers entering the labour force) and if only a few of the new members of the labour force find work, then the unemployment *rate* will rise but the number of employed will rise slightly.

2. The number of employed is a component of the labour force; information on that number can be obtained directly.

CHAPTER 10 The Monetary System

I. Chapter Overview

A. Context and Purpose

Chapter 10 is the first chapter in a two-chapter sequence dealing with money and prices in the long run. Chapter 10 describes what money is and develops how the Bank of Canada controls the quantity of money. Because changes in the quantity of money influence the rate of inflation in the long run, the following chapter concentrates on the causes and costs of inflation.

The purpose of Chapter 10 is to help develop an understanding of what money is, what forms money takes, how the banking system helps create money, and how the Bank of Canada controls the quantity of money. An understanding of money is important because changes in the quantity of money affect inflation and interest rates in the long run, and production and employment in the short run.

B. Helpful Hints

1. *Fiat money maintains value due to artificial scarcity.* Gold has value because people desire it for its intrinsic value and because it is naturally scarce (alchemists have never been able to create gold). However, fiat money is cheap and easy to produce. Therefore, fiat money maintains its value only because of self-restraint on the part of the producer. If Canadian dollars are a quality store of value, it is because the paper notes are difficult to counterfeit and the Bank of Canada shows self-restraint in the production of dollars.

2. *Paper notes and coins are considered "currency" only when in the hands of the nonbank public.* When economists use the word currency, they mean "currency in the hands of the nonbank public." When a person deposits currency in the bank, the person now owns a deposit, and the paper dollars are now the "reserves" of the bank. Currency in the hands of the nonbank public has decreased, while deposits have increased by an equal amount. At this point, the money supply is unaltered because money is the sum of currency (in the hands of the nonbank public) and deposits.

3. *The money multiplier is most easily understood in words.* If we state the relationship between reserves, deposits, and the multiplier in words, it clarifies the relationship. Because a fractional reserve system implies that "reserves are some fraction of deposits," it follows that "deposits are some multiple of reserves." For example, if reserves are one-fifth of deposits, then deposits are 5 times reserves. Because deposit expansion actually takes place due to banks lending some of their reserves, it is most useful to think "deposits are some multiple of reserves."

4. *When dealing with open-market operations, ask yourself, "Who pays?"* It is easiest to remember the impact of open-market operations by asking yourself, "Who pays?" When the Bank of Canada buys a government bond from the public, the Bank of Canada pays with "new dollars" and the money supply expands. When the Bank of Canada sells government bonds, the public pays with dollars and the Bank of Canada "retires" the dollars. That is, the dollars cease to exist when the Bank of Canada receives payment. Note that when the Bank of Canada sells bonds, it is not "issuing" bonds. It is selling existing bonds that were previously issued by the Government of Canada.

II. Self-Testing Challenges

A. True/False Questions

_____1.   Money and wealth are the same thing.

_____2.   Fiat money is Italy's national currency.

_____3.   Commodity money has value independent of its use as money.

_____4.   The M1+ money supply is composed of currency and demand deposits.

_____5.   When a person is willing to go to sleep tonight with $100 in his wallet, and he has complete confidence that he can spend it tomorrow and receive the same amount of goods as he would have received had he spent it today, money has demonstrated its function as a medium of exchange.

_____6.   Money has three functions: It acts as a medium of exchange, a unit of account, and a hedge against inflation.

_____7.   Credit cards are part of the M2 money supply.

_____8.   The Bank of Canada is Canada's central bank and is managed by a board of directors, which is appointed by the minister of Finance.

_____9.   The Bank of Canada and the U.S. Federal Reserve both relied on quantitative easing during the 2008–09 financial crisis.

_____10.   If there is 100 percent reserve banking, the money supply is unaffected by the proportion of dollars that the public chooses to hold as currency versus deposits.

_____11.   If the Bank of Canada purchases $100 000 of government bonds, and the reserve ratio is 10 percent, the maximum increase in the money supply is $10 000.

_____12.   If the Bank of Canada desires to contract the money supply, it could raise the overnight rate.

_____13.   If the leverage ratio is 20, a 5 percent fall in the value of a bank's assets leads to a 100 percent fall in bank capital.

_____14.   The Bank of Canada sterilizes foreign exchange purchases by buying government bonds.

_____15.   If banks choose to hold extra reserves, lending decreases and the money supply decreases.

B. Multiple-Choice Questions

1.   Which one of the following is **NOT** a function of money?
   a.   store of value
   b.   unit of account
   c.   medium of exchange
   d.   hedge against inflation

2.   Which one of the following describes the composition of M1+ money?
   a.   currency and demand deposits
   b.   currency, government bonds, and coins
   c.   currency, savings accounts, and government bonds
   d.   currency, demand deposits, and money market mutual funds

3.   Which one of the following is an example of fiat money?
   a.   gold
   b.   silver
   c.   paper dollars
   d.   cigarettes in a prisoner-of-war camp

4.   Which one of the following is **NOT** a function of the Bank of Canada?
   a.   issue currency
   b.   act as banker to the commercial banks
   c.   act as banker to the federal government
   d.   insure the deposits of the public at Canadian banks

5.   Which of the following is a characteristic of commodity money?
   a.   has intrinsic value
   b.   has no intrinsic value
   c.   is used exclusively in Canada
   d.   is used as reserves to back fiat money

6.   Which one of the following describes how the governor of the Bank of Canada is insulated from short-term political pressure?
   a.   The governor has life-time tenure.
   b.   The governor is elected by the public.
   c.   The governor is appointed to a seven-year term.
   d.   The governor is supervised by the finance committee of parliament.

7.   Which one of the following statements is true?
   a.   The Bank of Canada currently uses the overnight rate for control of the money supply.
   b.   Quantitative easing is when the Bank of Canada buys and sells Treasury bills.
   c.   Leverage is the process of offsetting foreign exchange market operations with open-market operations.
   d.   The Bank of Canada has frequently used changes in reserve requirements to control the money supply.

8.   National Bank has $4000 in reserves, $16 000 in loans, $18 000 in deposits, and $2000 in bank capital. Which one of the following is the leverage ratio for National Bank?
   a.   2
   b.   8
   c.   9
   d.   10

9.   If the reserve ratio is 2 percent, which one of the following is the value of the money multiplier?
   a.   2
   b.   4
   c.   10
   d.   50

10.   Which one of the following policy actions by the Bank of Canada would likely increase the money supply?
   a.   raising reserve requirements
   b.   selling government bonds
   c.   decreasing the overnight rate
   d.   selling foreign currency

11.   Suppose the Bank of Canada buys US$200 million in the foreign exchange market for CDN$215 million. Which one of the following describes how the Bank of Canada would sterilize this foreign exchange market operation?
   a.   It would lower the overnight rate.
   b.   It would raise the overnight rate.
   c.   It would buy government bonds on the open market.
   d.   It would sell government bonds on the open market.

12. Which one of the following is an outcome of a decrease in the reserve ratio?
    a. reserves rise
    b. money supply falls
    c. money multiplier rises
    d. banks reduce their loans

13. Which of the following defines the bank rate?
    a. the interest rate banks pay on the public's deposits
    b. the interest rate the Bank of Canada charges on loans to banks
    c. the interest rate the Bank of Canada pays on the public's deposits
    d. the interest rate the public pays when borrowing from banks

14. Suppose Glenda writes a $1000 cheque on her account to buy a government bond from her friend Anthony. If Anthony deposits the cheque in his bank, and if the reserve ratio is 20 percent, which one of the following is the potential change in the money supply?
    a. zero
    b. $1000
    c. $4000
    d. $5000

15. Suppose the Bank of Canada purchases a $1000 government bond from Hiroko. If Hiroko deposits the entire $1000 in her bank, and if the reserve ratio is 20 percent, which one of the following is the potential change in the money supply as a result of the Bank of Canada's action?
    a. zero
    b. $1000
    c. $4000
    d. $5000

16. Suppose all banks maintain a 100 percent reserve ratio. Which one of the following would be the outcome if an individual deposits $1000 of currency in a bank?
    a. The money supply is unaffected.
    b. The money supply increases by more than $1000.
    c. The money supply increases by less than $1000.
    d. The money supply decreases by $1000.

17. Suppose the Bank of Canada raises the overnight rate. Which one of the following would be the outcome?
    a. The money supply should rise.
    b. The money supply should fall.
    c. The money supply should remain unchanged.
    d. It is uncertain what would happen to the money supply.

18.   Given the following T-account, and assuming the reserve ratio is 5 percent, which one of the following is the largest new loan this bank can prudently make?

<u>National Bank</u>

<u>Assets</u>	<u>Liabilities</u>
Reserves $250	Deposits $1000
Loans $750	

a. $0
b. $50
c. $150
d. $200

19.   Which one of the following describes the three main tools of monetary policy?
a. coin, currency, and demand deposits
b. the money supply, government purchases, and taxation
c. government expenditures, taxation, and reserve requirements
d. open-market operations, reserve requirements, and the overnight rate

20.   Suppose the Bank of Canada purchases a government bond from a person who deposits the entire amount from the sale into his bank. If the bank holds some of the deposit as excess reserves, which one of the following describes what will happen to the money supply?
a. It will rise less than the money multiplier would suggest.
b. It will rise more than the money multiplier would suggest.
c. It will fall less than the money multiplier would suggest.
d. It will fall more than the money multiplier would suggest.

C. Short-Answer Questions

1.   What is barter, and why does it limit trade? _____
_____
_____

2.   What are the three functions of money? _____
_____
_____

3.   What are the two basic kinds of money? _____
_____

4.   In Canada, what two main assets are clearly money, and how do they differ from all other assets? (that is, define money) _____
_____
_____
_____

5. What are the four main jobs of the Bank of Canada? _____
    _____
    _____
    _____

6. What are the three monetary policy tools of the Bank of Canada? Which one does
    the Bank of Canada currently use to control the money supply?
    _____
    _____
    _____

7. What is the Basel III agreement? _____
    _____
    _____
    _____

8. If the Bank of Canada buys $1000 of government bonds from Justin, and he holds
    all the payment as currency at home, by how much does the money supply rise?
    _____
    _____

9. If the Bank of Canada buys $1000 of government bonds from Nicholas, and he
    deposits the entire $1000 in a demand deposit at his bank, and banks have a 10
    percent reserve ratio, by how much could the money supply increase?
    _____

10. Suppose the reserve ratio is 5 percent. If Lucille writes a cheque on her account at
    Bank 1 to buy a $1000 government bond from her roommate Sandra, and Sandra
    deposits the $1000 in her account at Bank 2, by how much will the money supply
    change? _____
    _____
    _____

11. Suppose there is no deposit insurance. Suppose rumours circulate that banks have
    made many bad loans and may be unable to repay their depositors. Describe what
    depositors and banks would be expected to do, and what their behaviour would do
    to the money supply. _____
    _____
    _____
    _____

D. Practice Problems

1. Suppose the Bank of Canada purchases a Government of Canada bond from Pierre for $10 000.

   a. What is the name of the Bank of Canada's action? _____
   _____

   b. Suppose Pierre deposits the $10 000 in First Student Bank. Show this transaction on First Student Bank's T-account.

   <u>First Student Bank</u>

<u>Assets</u>	<u>Liabilities</u>

   c. Suppose First Student Bank decides to keep 20 percent of its deposits on reserve and to loan out the rest. Show this transaction on the T-account.

   <u>First Student Bank</u>

<u>Assets</u>	<u>Liabilities</u>

   d. At this point, how much money has been created from the Bank of Canada's policy action? _____
   _____

   e. What is the value of the money multiplier? _____
   _____

   f. After infinite rounds of depositing and lending, how much money could be created from the Bank of Canada's policy action? _____
   _____
   _____

   g. If, during the rounds of depositing and lending, some people keep some extra currency and fail to deposit all their receipts, will there be more or less money created from the Bank of Canada's policy action than you found in part (f)? Why? _____
   _____
   _____

   h. If, during the rounds of depositing and lending, some banks choose to hold some of the money as extra reserves, will there be more or less money created from the Bank of Canada's policy action than you found in part (f)? Why?
   _____
   _____

2. Suppose the entire economy contains $1000 worth of five-dollar Bank of Canada notes.

   a. If people fail to deposit any of the dollars but instead hold all $1000 as currency, how large is the money supply? Explain. _____

   _____

   _____

   b. If people deposit the entire $1000 in banks that have a 100 percent reserve ratio, how large is the money supply? Explain. _____

   _____

   _____

   c. If people deposit the entire $1000 in banks that have a 20 percent reserve ratio, how large could the money supply become? Explain. _____

   _____

   _____

   d. In part (c), what portion of the money supply was created due to the banks? (Hint: $1000 of notes already existed.)_____

   _____

   _____

   e. If people deposit the entire $1000 in banks that have a 10 percent reserve ratio, how large could the money supply become? _____

   _____

   f. Compare your answer in part (e) to part (c). Explain why they are different.

   _____

   _____

   _____

   g. Suppose people deposit the entire $1000 in banks that have a 10 percent reserve ratio. One day, however, the bankers become more cautious about economic conditions. They decide to make fewer loans and hold another 10 percent of deposits as extra reserves. How large could the money supply become? _____

   _____

   _____

   h. Compare your answer in part (c) to part (g). Are these answers the same? Why or why not? _____

   _____

   _____

E. Advanced Critical Thinking

Suppose Mark is a personal friend of the governor of the Bank of Canada. The governor comes over to Mark's house for lunch and notices Mark's desk. The governor is so struck by the beauty of the desk that he simply must have it for his office. He buys it for $1000 and, because it is for his office, he pays with a cheque drawn on the Bank of Canada.

1. Are there more dollars in the economy than before? Why or why not?

    _____

    _____

2. Why does the Bank of Canada not buy and sell desks, real estate, and so on, instead of government bonds, when it desires to change the money supply?

    _____

    _____

    _____

3. If the Bank of Canada does not want the money supply to rise when it purchases new furniture, what might it do to offset the purchase? _____

    _____

    _____

III. Solutions

A. True/False Questions

1. F; money is the spendable portion of one's wealth.
2. F; fiat money is money without intrinsic value.
3. T
4. T
5. F; money demonstrated its function as a store of value.
6. F; store of value, not a hedge against inflation.
7. F; credit cards are not included in the money supply.
8. T
9. F; the Bank of Canada did not need to rely on quantitative easing.
10. T
11. F; the maximum increase in the money supply is $100\ 000 \times (1/0.10) =$ $1\ 000\ 000.
12. T
13. T
14. F; foreign exchange purchases are sterilized by selling government bonds.
15. T

B. Multiple-Choice Questions

1. d	5. a	9. d	13. b	17. b
2. a	6. c	10. c	14. a	18. d
3. c	7. a	11. d	15. d	19. d
4. d	8. d	12. c	16. a	20. a

C. Short-Answer Questions

1. Barter is trading goods and services directly for other goods and services. It requires a double coincidence of wants.

2. The three functions of money are medium of exchange, unit of account, and store of value.

3. The two basic kinds of money are commodity money and fiat money.

4. Canada's two main money assets are currency and demand deposits. They are the assets that are directly spendable and are commonly accepted in trade for goods and services.

5. The four main jobs of the Bank of Canada are to issue currency, to act as banker to the commercial banks, to act as banker to the Canadian government, and to control the quantity of money in the economy.

6. The three monetary policy tools of the Bank of Canada are open-market operations, reserve requirements, and the overnight rate. The Bank of Canada currently uses the overnight rate to control the money supply.

7. It is an international agreement in response to the financial crisis of 2008-2009 that requires central banks to impose higher minimum capital requirements on their national banks.

8. The money supply rises by $1000.

9. The money supply could increase by $10 000 (that is, $1000 \times (1/.10) = \$10\ 000$).

10. The money supply will not change at all. In this case, reserves are only moved from one bank to another.

11. Depositors will withdraw their deposits, thus reducing bank reserves. Banks will try to hold extra reserves to prepare for the deposit withdrawal. Both will reduce bank lending and the money supply.

D. Practice Problems

1. a.   The name of the action is open-market operations.

    b.

    #### First Student Bank

Assets	Liabilities
Reserves $10 000	Deposits $10 000

    c.

    #### First Student Bank

Assets	Liabilities
Reserves $2000	
Loans $8000	Deposits $10 000

    d.   The amount created so far is $18 000 (that is, $10 000 + $8000 = $18 000).

    e.   The value of the multiplier is 5 (that is, 1/0.20 = 5).

    f.   The amount of money that could be created is $50 000 (that is, $10 000 × 5 = $50 000).

    g.   Less money will be created because a smaller amount of each loan gets redeposited to be available for loan again.

    h.   Less money will be created because a smaller amount of each deposit gets loaned out to be available for deposit again.

2. a.   The size of the money supply is $1000 because there is $1000 in currency and $0 in deposits.

    b.   The size of the money supply is $1000 because there is now $0 in currency and $1000 in deposits.

    c.   The money supply could become $5000 (that is, $1000 × (1/0.20) = $5000) because $1000 of new reserves can support $5000 worth of deposits.

    d.   The potential money supply is $5000, but $1000 was currency already in the system. Thus, an additional $4000 was created by the banks.

    e.   The money supply could become $10 000 (that is, $1000 × (1/0.10) = $10 000).

    f.   Banks can create more money from the same amount of new reserves when the reserve ratio is lower because they can lend a larger portion of each new deposit.

g.   The money supply could become $5000 (that is, $1000 × 1/(0.10 + 0.10) = $5000).

h.   Yes, they are the same. With respect to deposit creation, it does not matter why banks hold reserves. It only matters how much they hold.

E. Advanced Critical Thinking

1.   Yes. When the Bank of Canada purchases anything, they pay with newly created dollars, which puts more dollars in the economy.

2.   The transaction costs and storage costs would be staggering. Also, the value of the inventory of "items" would never be certain. The open market for government bonds is much more efficient.

3.   The Bank of Canada could sell government bonds of equal value to offset the purchase.

CHAPTER 11 | Money Growth and Inflation

I. Chapter Overview

A. Context and Purpose

Chapter 11 is the second chapter in a two-chapter sequence dealing with money and prices in the long run. Chapter 10 explained what money is and how the Bank of Canada controls the quantity of money. Chapter 11 establishes the relationship between the rate of growth of money and the inflation rate.

The purpose of this chapter is to explain the causes and costs of inflation. It is shown that, in the long run, there is a strong relationship between the growth rate of money and inflation. It is also shown that there are numerous costs to the economy from high inflation, but that there is not a consensus on the size of these costs when inflation is moderate.

B. Helpful Hints

1. *The price of money is 1/P.* Because the price of goods and services is measured in terms of money, the price of money is measured in terms of the quantity of goods and services for which money can be exchanged. For example, if a basket of goods and services costs $5, then $P = \$5$. The price of a dollar is then $1/P$ or one-fifth of the basket of goods. That is, one dollar exchanges for one-fifth of the basket of goods. If the price of the basket of goods doubles such that it now sells for $10, the price of money has fallen to one-half its original value. Numerically, because the price of the basket is now $10, or $P = \$10$, the price of money has fallen to $1/P$ or one-tenth of the basket of goods. To summarize, when the price of a $5 basket of goods and services doubles, the price of money falls by half; that is, it falls to one-tenth of the basket of goods.

2. *When dealing with the quantity theory, imagine being at an auction.* At the end of the auction, the number of items sold and the average price of each item sold are calculated. Suppose the auction is repeated, only now the doorman doubles the money each buyer takes into the auction—a buyer that had $20 now has $40, and so on. If all participants spend the same percent of their money as at the prior auction (equivalent to a constant velocity), and if the items available to buy are unchanged (equivalent to a constant real output), what must happen to the average price of goods sold at the auction? Prices at the auction will precisely double, showing that prices are proportional to the quantity of money.

3. *Unexpected inflation works like a tax on future receipts.* Unexpected inflation redistributes wealth. Although it can be difficult to remember who wins and who loses on nominal contracts through time, things can always be kept straight by remembering that *unexpected inflation works like a tax on future receipts and like a subsidy to future payments.* Therefore, when inflation turns out to be higher than anticipated when a loan contract was written, the recipient of the future payments is worse off because he receives dollars with less purchasing power than he had bargained for. The person who borrowed is better off because he was able to use the money when it had greater value, yet was allowed to repay the loan with money of lower value. When inflation is higher than expected, wealth is redistributed from lenders to borrowers. When inflation is less than expected, winners and losers are reversed.

This concept can be applied to any contract that extends through time. Consider a labour contract. Recall, when inflation is greater than expected, those who receive money in the future are harmed and those who pay are helped. Therefore, firms gain at the expense of workers when inflation is greater than anticipated. When inflation is less than expected, winners and losers are reversed.

II. Self-Testing Challenges

A. True/False Questions

_____1.   An increase in the price level is the same as a decrease in the value of money.

_____2.   The quantity theory of money suggests that an increase in the money supply increases real output proportionately.

_____3.   If the price level were to double, the quantity of money demanded would double because people would need twice as much money to cover the same transactions.

_____4.   In the long run, an increase in the money supply tends to have an effect on real variables but no effect on nominal variables.

_____5.   If the money supply is $300, real output is 2400 units, and the average price of 1 unit of real output is $4, then the velocity of money is 32.

_____6.   The Fisher effect suggests that, in the long run, if the rate of inflation rises from 2 percent to 5 percent, the nominal interest rate should increase by 5 percentage points and the real interest rate should remain unchanged.

_____7.   An inflation tax is "paid" by those that hold money because inflation reduces the value of their money holdings.

_____8.   Monetary neutrality means that a change in the money supply does not cause a change in anything at all.

_____9.   The costs of deflation are minor compared to the costs of inflation.

_____10.   Inflation reduces the relative price of those goods for which the price has been temporarily held constant to avoid the costs associated with changing prices.

_____11.   The shoeleather costs of inflation should be approximately the same for a medical doctor and for an unemployed worker.

_____12.   Inflation tends to stimulate saving because it raises the after-tax real return to saving.

_____13.   Countries that spend more money than they can collect from taxing or borrowing tend to print too much money, and this causes inflation.

_____14.   The costs of hyperinflation can include corruption, human rights violations, and poverty.

_____15.   The Bank of Canada has an inflation target of 2 percent.

B. Multiple-Choice Questions

1.   In the long run, which one of the following is a cause of inflation?
   a. governments that print too much money
   b. increases in the price of inputs, such as labour and oil
   c. banks that have market power and refuse to lend money
   d. governments that raise taxes so high that the cost of doing business increases and, hence, the prices also increase

2.   Which one of the following terms refers to prices rising at an extraordinarily high rate?
   a. inflation
   b. deflation
   c. hyperinflation
   d. disinflation

3.   Which one of the following occurs if the price level doubles?
   a. Nominal income is unaffected.
   b. The money supply has been cut by half.
   c. The value of money has been cut by half.
   d. The quantity demanded of money falls by half.

4. In the long run, which one of the following is the demand for money **MOST** dependent upon?
   a. the interest rate
   b. the level of prices
   c. the availability of credit cards
   d. the availability of banking outlets

5. Which one of the following is the conclusion of the quantity theory of money?
   a. An increase in the money supply causes a proportional increase in velocity.
   b. An increase in the money supply causes a proportional increase in prices.
   c. An increase in the money supply causes a proportional increase in real output.
   d. An increase in the money supply causes a proportional decrease in velocity.

6. Which one of the following is an example of a real variable?
   a. the dollar wage
   b. the price of corn
   c. the nominal interest rate
   d. the ratio of the price of milk to the price of bread

7. Which one of the following is the quantity equation?
   a. money × price level = velocity × real output
   b. money × real output = velocity × price level
   c. money × velocity = price level × real output

8. If money is neutral, which of the following can be assumed?
   a. An increase in the money supply does nothing.
   b. A change in the money supply affects only real variables, such as real output.
   c. The money supply cannot be changed because it is tied to a commodity, such as gold.
   d. A change in the money supply affects only nominal variables, such as prices and dollar wages.

9. If the money supply grows by 7 percent and real output grows by 4 percent, and velocity is constant, which one of the following is the amount that prices should rise by?
   a. 0 percent
   b. 3 percent
   c. 7 percent
   d. 11 percent

10. Which one of the following defines velocity?
    a. the annual unstable output
    b. the annual rate of turnover of output
    c. the annual rate of turnover of the money supply
    d. the annual rate of turnover of business inventories

11. Which one of the following is a reason that a country would employ an inflation tax?
a. The government has a balanced budget.
b. An inflation tax is the most equitable of all taxes.
c. The government does not understand the causes and consequences of inflation.
d. Government expenditures are high and the government has inadequate tax collections and difficulty borrowing.

12. Which of the following is characteristic of an inflation tax?
a. a tax on people who hold money
b. usually employed by governments with balanced budgets
c. a tax on people who hold interest-bearing savings accounts
d. an explicit tax paid quarterly by businesses based on the amount of increase in the prices of their products

13. Suppose the nominal interest rate is 7 percent while the money supply is growing at a rate of 5 percent per year. If the government increases the growth rate of the money supply from 5 percent to 9 percent, which of the following should the nominal interest rate become, in the long run, according to the Fisher effect?
a. 4 percent
b. 9 percent
c. 11 percent
d. 12 percent

14. If the nominal interest rate is 6 percent and the inflation rate is 3 percent, which one of the following is the real interest rate?
a. 3 percent
b. 6 percent
c. 9 percent
d. 18 percent

15. Which one of the following occurs if actual inflation turns out to be greater than people expected?
a. No redistribution occurs.
b. The real interest rate is unaffected.
c. Wealth is redistributed to lenders from borrowers.
d. Wealth is redistributed to borrowers from lenders.

16. Which one of the following costs of inflation does not occur when inflation is constant and predictable?
a. menu costs
b. shoeleather costs
c. arbitrary redistributions of wealth
d. costs due to inflation-induced tax distortions

17.   Suppose that, because of inflation, a business in Pakistan must calculate, print, and mail a new price list to its customers each month. Which one of the following is this an example of?
   a.   menu costs
   b.   shoeleather costs
   c.   arbitrary redistributions of wealth
   d.   costs due to inflation-induced tax distortions

18.   Suppose that, because of inflation, people in Venezuela economize on currency and go to the bank each day to withdraw their daily currency needs. Which one of the following is this an example of?
   a.   menu costs
   b.   shoeleather costs
   c.   costs due to inflation-induced tax distortions
   d.   costs due to inflation-induced relative price variability that misallocates resources

19.   If the real interest rate is 4 percent, the inflation rate is 6 percent, and the tax rate is 20 percent, which one of the following is the after-tax real interest rate?
   a.   1 percent
   b.   2 percent
   c.   3 percent
   d.   4 percent

20.   Which one of the following statements is true about a situation where real incomes are rising at 2 percent per year?
   a.   If inflation were 0 percent, people should receive raises of about 0 percent.
   b.   If inflation were 5 percent, people should receive raises of about 2 percent per year.
   c.   If inflation were 5 percent, people should receive raises of about 5 percent per year.
   d.   If inflation were 5 percent, people should receive raises of about 7 percent per year.

C. Short-Answer Questions

1.   If the money supply doubles, what must happen in the long run to the quantity of money demanded and to the price level? _____

_____

_____

_____

2.   Explain the classical dichotomy. _____

_____

_____

3. Within the framework of the classical dichotomy, which type of variable is affected by changes in money and which type is not? What phrase do we use to capture this effect? _____

_____

4. How does unexpected deflation redistribute wealth? _____

_____

_____

5. Suppose the money supply were to increase by 10 percent. Explain what would happen to each variable in the quantity equation? _____

_____

_____

6. What are the three sources of revenue a government can use to support its expenditures? Which method causes inflation, and who bears the burden of this method of raising revenue? _____

_____

_____

7. In the long run, what does an increase in the growth rate of the money supply do to real and nominal interest rates? _____ _____

_____

_____

8. Does inflation erode the value of people's incomes and thereby lower their standard of living? Explain. _____

_____

9. What are the costs of inflation when inflation is perfectly anticipated?

_____

_____

10. Suppose inflation turns out to be lower than expected. Who is likely to gain, borrowers or lenders? Union workers or firms? Why? _____

_____

_____

11. What is the inconsistency in the following statement? "When inflation is high but stable and predictable, inflation does not redistribute wealth." _____

_____

12.   Since 1992, the Bank of Canada has successfully used monetary policy to keep inflation close to its 2 percent target. Explain how the Bank of Canada does this.

_____

_____

_____

_____

D. Practice Problems

1.   Use the quantity equation for this problem. Suppose the money supply is $200, real output is 1000 units, and the price per unit of output is $1.

a.   What is the value of velocity? _____

_____

b.   If velocity is fixed at the value you solved for in part (a), what does the quantity theory of money suggest will happen if the money supply is increased to $400? _____

_____

_____

c.   Is your answer in part (b) consistent with the classical dichotomy? Explain.

_____

_____

_____

d.   Suppose that when the money supply is doubled (that is, to $400), real output grows a small amount (say 2 percent). Now what will happen to prices? Do prices more than double, less than double, or exactly double? Why?

_____

_____

_____

e.   When inflation gets very high, people do not like to hold money because it is losing value quickly. Therefore, they spend it faster. If, when the money supply is doubled, people spend money more quickly, what happens to prices? Do prices more than double, less than double, or exactly double? Why?

_____

_____

f.   Suppose the money supply at the beginning of this problem refers to M1+. That is, the M1+ money supply is $200. What would the M2 quantity equation look like if the M2 money supply were $500 (and all other values were as stated at the beginning of the problem)? _____

_____

2. The following questions are related to the Fisher effect.

    a. To demonstrate understanding of the Fisher effect, complete the following table.

Real interest rate	Nominal interest rate	Expected inflation rate
3%	10%	_____
_____	6%	2%
5%	_____	3%

The following questions are about the Fisher effect but **they are NOT related to the table above.**

    b. Suppose people expect inflation to be 3 percent, and suppose the desired real interest rate is 4 percent. What is the nominal rate? _____

    _____

    c. Suppose inflation turns out to be 6 percent. What is the actual real interest rate on loans that were signed based on the expectations in part (b)?

    _____

    _____

    d. Was wealth redistributed to the lender from the borrower or to the borrower from the lender, when inflation was expected to be 3 percent but, in fact, turned out to be 6 percent? _____ _____

    _____

    _____

    _____

    e. What would have happened had inflation turned out to be only 1 percent?

    _____

    _____

    _____

3.   Income taxes treat nominal interest earned on savings as income even though much of the nominal interest is just to compensate for inflation.

   a.   To see what this does to the incentive to save, complete the following table for both the low-inflation and high-inflation country.

	Low-inflation country	High-inflation country
Real interest rate	5%	5%
Inflation rate	3%	11%
Nominal interest rate	_____	_____
Reduced interest due to a 25% tax	_____	_____
After-tax nominal interest rate	_____	_____
After-tax real interest rate	_____	_____

   b.   In which country is there a greater incentive to save? Why? _____
   _____
   _____

   c.   What could the government do to eliminate this problem? _____
   _____

E. Advanced Critical Thinking

   Suppose Sandra explains the concept of an "inflation tax" to her friend Jordan. Sandra correctly tells him, "When a government prints money to cover its expenditures instead of taxing or borrowing, it causes inflation. An inflation tax is simply the erosion of the value of money from this inflation. Therefore, the burden of the tax lands on those who hold money." Jordan responds, "What's so bad about that? Rich people have all the money so an inflation tax seems fair to me. Maybe the government should finance all of its expenditures by printing money."

1.   Is it true that rich people hold more money than poor people? _____
   _____

2.   Do rich people hold a higher percent of their wealth as money than poor people?
   _____
   _____

3.   Does an inflation tax place a greater burden on the poor than on the rich? Why or why not? _____
   _____
   _____
   _____

4. Are there any other reasons why engaging in an inflation tax is not good policy?

_____

_____

_____

III. Solutions

A. True/False Questions

1. T
2. F; it increases the price level proportionately.
3. T
4. F; the money supply tends to have an effect on nominal variables but not on real variables.
5. T
6. F; the nominal interest rate should increase by 3 percentage points.
7. T
8. F; it does not cause a change in real variables.
9. F; deflation also has costs that are similar to those of inflation.
10. T
11. F; the opportunity costs of trips to the bank are greater for a medical doctor.
12. F; inflation tends to reduce the after-tax real return to saving.
13. T
14. T
15. T

B. Multiple-Choice Questions

1. a	5. b	9. b	13. c	17. a
2. c	6. d	10. c	14. a	18. b
3. c	7. c	11. d	15. d	19. b
4. b	8. d	12. a	16. c	20. d

C. Short-Answer Questions

1. The quantity of money demanded must double to maintain monetary equilibrium. Spending will double on the same amount of goods, thus causing prices to double and the value of money to fall by half.

2. Classical dichotomy is the view that macroeconomic variables can be divided into two groups: real (measured in physical units) and nominal (measured in monetary units).

3. Nominal are affected. Real are not. This effect is known as monetary neutrality.

4.   Unexpected deflation redistributes wealth from debtors, who are often poorer, to creditors, who are often wealthier.

5. V remains constant, Y remains constant, M rises by 10 percent, and P rises by 10 percent.

6.   taxes, borrowing, and printing money; printing money; those that hold money because its value decreases

7.   There is no impact on the real interest rate in the long run. It raises the nominal interest rate one-to-one with the increase in the growth rate of money and prices.

8.   No. Income is a result of selling labour services, the value of which rises along with other prices during an inflation.

9.   shoeleather costs, menu costs, costs due to relative-price variability that misallocates resources, tax distortions, confusion, and inconvenience

10.   lenders; workers. Those who receive dollars in the future on contract receive dollars of greater value than they had bargained for.

11.   When inflation is high, it is always unstable and difficult to predict.

12.   If the Bank of Canada thinks that inflation will rise above (fall below) the 2 percent target, it raises (lowers) the overnight rate of interest, which reduces (increases) the growth rate of the money supply, and reduces (increases) future inflation.

D. Practice Problems

1. a. $(1000 \times \$1)/\$200 = 5$

    b. $\$400 \times 5 = \$2 \times 1000$. Prices will double from \$1 to \$2

    c.   Yes. The classical dichotomy divides economic variables into real and nominal. Money affects nominal variables proportionately and has no impact on real variables. In part (b), prices double, but real output remains constant.

    d.   The quantity equation says that nominal output must change in proportion to the change in money. Prices will still rise, but because real output is larger, prices will less than double.

    e.   Money has a proportional impact on nominal output if V is constant. If V grows, a doubling of M will cause P to more than double.

    f. $\$500 \times 2 = \$1 \times 1000$. M2 velocity is 2.

2. a.

Real interest rate	Nominal interest rate	Expected inflation rate
3%	10%	<u>7%</u>
<u>4%</u>	6%	2%
5%	<u>8%</u>	3%

b. 3% + 4% = 7%

c. People would have signed loan contracts for 7 percent nominal interest. Therefore, 7% − 6% = 1%.

d. People expected a real interest rate of 4 percent, but the actual real interest rate turned out to be 1 percent. Wealth was redistributed to the borrower from the lender.

e. The original loan contract would be the same. Thus 7% − 1% = 6%. The actual real rate is 6 percent instead of 4 percent; therefore, wealth is redistributed to lenders from borrowers.

3. a.

	Low-inflation country	High-inflation country
Real interest rate	5%	5%
Inflation rate	3%	11%
Nominal interest rate	<u>8%</u>	<u>16%</u>
Reduced interest due to a 25% tax	<u>2%</u>	<u>4%</u>
After-tax nominal interest rate	<u>6%</u>	<u>12%</u>
After-tax real interest rate	<u>3%</u>	<u>1%</u>

b. There is a greater incentive to save in the low-inflation country because the after-tax real interest rate is larger.

c. They could eliminate inflation, or tax only real interest income.

E. Advanced Critical Thinking

1.   Yes, rich people probably hold more dollars than poor people.

2.   No, by a wide margin, the poor hold a larger percent of their wealth as money. In fact, a poor person may have no other financial assets at all.

3.   An inflation tax places a far greater burden on the poor than on the rich. The rich are able to keep most of their assets in inflation-adjusted, interest-bearing assets. This was observed in Brazil and Argentina during periods of high inflation.

4.   Inflation imposes many other costs on the economy besides the inflation tax: shoeleather costs, menu costs, tax distortions, confusion, resource misallocation, and wealth redistribution.

12 Open-Economy Macroeconomics: Basic Concepts

I. Chapter Overview

A. Context and Purpose

Chapter 12 is the first chapter in a two-chapter sequence dealing with open-economy macroeconomics. Chapter 12 develops the basic concepts and vocabulary associated with macroeconomics in an international setting: net exports, net capital outflow, real and nominal exchange rates, purchasing-power parity, and interest rate parity. The next chapter, Chapter 13, builds an open-economy macroeconomic model that shows how these variables are determined simultaneously.

The purpose of Chapter 12 is to develop the basic concepts macroeconomists use to study open economies. The chapter addresses why a nation's net exports must equal its net capital outflow. It also addresses the concepts of the real and nominal exchange rates, develops a theory of exchange rate determination known as purchasing-power parity, and discusses the relationship between Canadian and world interest rates.

B. Helpful Hints

1. *Negative net capital outflow increases domestic investment.* National saving is used to support domestic investment and net capital outflow:

    $$S = I + NCO.$$

    If *NCO* is negative, it means that foreigners invest more in Canada than Canadians invest abroad. This allows domestic investment to exceed Canada's national saving. For example, suppose saving is $150 billion and net capital outflow is –$20 billion. Domestic investment is $I = \$150 + \$20$, or $170 billion.

2. *Always express nominal and real exchange rates in terms of foreign units relative to domestic units.* Expressing exchange rates in terms of foreign units relative to domestic units helps avoid confusion because a rise in this exchange rate is associated with a rise in the value of the domestic unit. For example, suppose the nominal exchange rate between the yen and the dollar is expressed as 100 yen per dollar. If the exchange rate rises to 110 yen per dollar, the value of the dollar has risen.

3. *When generating nominal or real exchange rate, always identify the units of measurement.* A common mistake committed by students when calculating exchange rates (particularly real exchange rates) is to fail to identify the units of measurement throughout the problem and to try to attach the units of

measurement at the end of the problem after a numerical solution has been found. This leaves much room for error and confusion. Notice in the real exchange rate example in the textbook about Russian and Canadian wheat that the units are attached to the numbers throughout. This is not just for your convenience. It is necessary to attach all the units to avoid making mistakes, even if a person has much experience in doing the calculations.

4. *Purchasing-power parity should hold for goods of high value and low transportation costs.* The law of one price applies to goods for which arbitrage is most likely. Hence, we might expect the dollar price of diamonds to be the same in all countries because small deviations in the price of diamonds create substantial profit opportunities. However, large deviations in prices of shoeshines between Vancouver and New York City are unlikely to create profit opportunities nor a movement of goods or services. Expected future growth in the production and trade of high-technology, high-value products should increase the applicability of the purchasing-power parity theory.

II. Self-Testing Challenges

A. True/False Questions

_____1.   Net exports are defined as imports minus exports.

_____2.   Canadian net capital outflow falls when a German pension fund buys stock in TransCanada Pipelines Limited.

_____3.   For any country, net exports are always equal to net capital outflow because every international transaction involves an exchange of an equal value of some combination of goods and/or assets.

_____4.   For a given amount of Canadian national saving, an increase in Canadian net capital outflow decreases Canadian domestic investment.

_____5.   The current account balance measures net exports plus the net inflow of interest and dividend payments.

_____6.   A country that exports more than it imports is said to have a trade deficit.

_____7.   If the yen-per-dollar exchange rate rises, the dollar has appreciated.

_____8.   If a case of Coke costs $12 in Canada and 1800 yen in Japan, then according to the purchasing-power parity theory of exchange rates, the yen-per-dollar exchange rate should be 100 yen per dollar.

_____9.   If purchasing-power parity holds, then the real exchange rate is constant.

_____10.   If Mexico's money supply grows faster than Japan's, the value of the peso should rise relative to the value of the yen.

_____11.   If the nominal exchange rate is 3 euros to the Canadian dollar, and if the price of a Big Mac is $4 in Canada and 8 euros in Germany, then the real exchange rate is two-thirds German Big Mac per one Canadian Big Mac.

_____12.   In order to increase domestic investment, a country must either increase its saving or decrease its net capital outflow.

_____13.   Arbitrage is the process of taking advantage of differences in prices of the same good by buying it from a market where the good is cheap and selling it in another market where the good is expensive.

_____14.   Canadian real interest rates have been higher than U.S. real interest rates partly because of higher tax rates in Canada.

_____15.   One of the benefits of a common currency, like the Euro, is that each nation can still have its own monetary policy.

B. Multiple-Choice Questions

1.   Which one of the following terms refers to an economy that interacts with other economies?
   a.   a balanced trade economy
   b.   an export economy
   c.   an import economy
   d.   an open economy

2.   Which one of the following is **NOT** a reason why the Canadian economy continues to engage in greater amounts of international trade?
   a.   There are larger cargo ships and airplanes.
   b.   High-technology goods are more valuable per kilogram, and thus more likely to be traded.
   c.   NAFTA imposes requirements for increased trade between countries in North America.
   d.   There have been improvements in technology that have improved telecommunications between countries.

3.   Which one of the following statements is true about a country with a trade deficit?
   a.   Net exports are negative.
   b.   Exports exceed imports.
   c.   Net capital outflow must be positive.
   d.   The current account balance must be positive.

4. Which one of the following developments would directly increase Canadian net capital outflow?
   a. Honda builds a new plant in Ontario.
   b. Air Canada buys a new plane from the United States.
   c. Toyota buys stock in the Bank of Montreal.
   d. BlackBerry builds a new distribution facility in Sweden.

5. Which one of the following is correct if Japan exports more than it imports?
   a. Japan is running a trade deficit.
   b. Japan's net exports are negative.
   c. Japan's net capital outflow must be positive.
   d. Japan's current account balance must be negative

6. If Canada saves $200 billion and Canadian net capital outflow is −$35 billion, what is the value of Canadian domestic investment?
   a. −$35 billion
   b. $35 billion
   c. $165 billion
   d. $235 billion

7. Which one of the following is true if the exchange rate changes from 3 Euros per dollar to 4 Euros per dollar?
   a. The dollar has depreciated.
   b. The dollar has appreciated.
   c. The dollar could have appreciated or depreciated depending on what happened to relative prices in Europe and Canada.

8. Suppose the real exchange rate between Russia and Canada is defined in terms of bottles of Russian vodka per bottle of Canadian vodka. Which one of the following will increase the real exchange rate (i.e., increase the number of bottles of Russian vodka per bottle of Canadian vodka)?
   a. An increase in the ruble price of Russian vodka.
   b. An increase in the dollar price of Canadian vodka.
   c. A decrease in the number of rubles for which the dollar can be exchanged.

9. Which one of the following is the **MOST** accurate measure of the international value of the dollar?
   a. the yen-per-dollar exchange rate
   b. the euro-per-dollar exchange rate
   c. the U.S.-dollar-per-Canadian-dollar exchange rate
   d. an exchange rate index that accounts for many exchange rates

10. If the nominal exchange rate between British pounds and Canadian dollars is 0.8 pounds per dollar, which one of the following is the amount of Canadian dollars you can get for a British pound?
   a. 0.2 of a dollar
   b. 0.8 of a dollar
   c. 1.2 dollars
   d. 1.25 dollars

11. Suppose the nominal exchange rate between the Mexican peso and the Canadian dollar is 10 pesos per dollar. Further, suppose that a kilogram of hamburger costs $2 in Canada and 25 pesos in Mexico. Which one of the following is the real exchange rate between Mexico and Canada?
   a. 0.5 kg of Mexican hamburger per 1 kg of Canadian hamburger
   b. 0.8 kg of Mexican hamburger per 1 kg of Canadian hamburger
   c. 1.25 kg of Mexican hamburger per 1 kg of Canadian hamburger
   d. 2.5 kg of Mexican hamburger per 1 kg of Canadian hamburger

12. Which one of the following people would be pleased by a depreciation of the Canadian dollar?
   a. a Canadian tourist traveling in Europe
   b. a Canadian importer of Russian vodka
   c. a French exporter of wine to Canada
   d. an Italian importer of Canadian steel

13. Suppose a pastry costs 3.6 Euros in France and $1.40 in Canada. If purchasing-power parity holds, which one of the following is the nominal exchange rate between Euros and dollars?
   a. 0.39 Euros per dollar
   b. 1.00 Euro per dollar
   c. 2.57 Euros per dollar
   d. 5.00 Euros per dollar

14. Which one of the following products would likely be the **LEAST** accurate if used to calculate purchasing-power parity?
   a. gold
   b. automobiles
   c. diamonds
   d. dental services

15. Suppose the money supply in Mexico grows more quickly than the money supply in Canada. Which one of the following is the expected result?
   a. The peso should depreciate relative to the dollar.
   b. The peso should appreciate relative to the dollar.
   c. The peso should maintain a constant exchange rate with the dollar because of purchasing-power parity.

16. Suppose a resident of Canada buys a Jaguar automobile from Great Britain, and the British exporter uses the receipts to buy stock in Toronto Dominion Bank. Which one of the following statements is true from the perspective of Canada?
    a. Net exports fall and net capital outflow falls.
    b. Net exports rise and net capital outflow rises.
    c. Net exports fall and net capital outflow rises.
    d. Net exports rise and net capital outflow falls.

17. Which one of the following statements is **NOT** true about the relationship between national saving, investment, and net capital outflow?
    a. Saving is the sum of investment and net capital outflow.
    b. For a given amount of saving, an increase in net capital outflow must decrease domestic investment.
    c. For a given amount of saving, a decrease in net capital outflow must decrease domestic investment.
    d. An increase in saving associated with an equal increase in net capital outflow leaves domestic investment unchanged.

18. Suppose the inflation rate over the past 20 years has been 9 percent in Great Britain, 7 percent in Japan, and 5 percent in Canada. If purchasing-power parity holds, which one of the following statements describes the most likely result?
    a. Over this period, the value of the dollar should have fallen compared to the value of the pound and the yen.
    b. Over this period, the yen should have risen in value compared to the pound and fallen compared to the dollar.
    c. Over this period, the yen should have fallen in value compared to the pound and risen compared to the dollar.
    d. Over this period, the value of the pound should have risen compared to the value of the yen and the dollar.

19. If the interest rate in Canada equals the interest rate prevailing in world financial markets, which one of the following is this a result of?
    a. net exports
    b. net capital outflow
    c. interest rate parity
    d. purchasing-power parity

20. If the world interest rate is 6 percent and foreigners believe that there is a higher default risk in Canada, then what is the expected interest rate in Canada?
    a. more than 6 percent
    b. 6 percent
    c. less than 6 percent

C. Short-Answer Questions

1. Identify four reasons why the Canadian economy has engaged in an increasing amount of trade over the past 50 years. _____

    _____

    _____

2. Define net capital outflow. When foreigners invest in Canada, what happens to the value of Canadian *NCO*? _____

    _____

    _____

3. What are the two mutually exclusive locations where national saving can be invested? _____

    _____

4. If national saving is held constant, what happens to domestic investment if *NCO* decreases? Why? _____

    _____

    _____

5. Define the current account balance. When foreigners receive interest and dividends on their holdings of Canadian bonds and stocks, what happens to the current account balance? _____

    _____

    _____

6. In terms of the real exchange rate, what three variables could change to make Canada more competitive internationally? _____

    _____

    _____

7. Suppose a Ford Escort sells for CDN$20 000 in Canada, and for US$18 000 in the United States. If purchasing-power parity holds, how many Canadian dollars does it take to buy one US dollar? _____

    _____

8. What are the two reasons why purchasing-power parity does not always hold in practice? _____

    _____

    _____

    _____

9.   If the money supply grows at an average annual rate of 5 percent in Canada and at an average annual rate of 35 percent in Mexico, what should happen over time to the Mexican-peso-per-dollar exchange rate if purchasing-power parity holds? Why? _____

_____

_____

10.   Why might the interest rate in Canada be higher than the interest rate prevailing in world financial markets? _____

_____

D. Practice Problems

1.   How would each of the following transactions affect Canadian *NCO*? Does the transaction affect foreign direct investment or foreign portfolio investment?

a.   A Canadian mutual fund buys stock in American Airlines.

_____

b.   Bombardier buys steel from a Japanese manufacturer to use in the production of airplanes. _____

_____

_____

c.   Honda expands its plant in Ontario. _____

_____

d.   A Japanese mutual fund buys shares of stock in Royal Bank.

_____

e.   BlackBerry builds an office in Germany.

_____

2.   Suppose a resident of Great Britain buys a computer from a Canadian manufacturer using British pounds.

a.   If the Canadian manufacturer holds on to the British pounds, does $NX = NCO$ in this case? Explain. _____

_____

_____

b.   Suppose the Canadian manufacturer uses the pounds to help build a factory in Great Britain. Does $NX = NCO$ in this case? Explain. What kind of foreign investment is this? _____

_____

_____

c. Suppose the Canadian manufacturer uses the pounds to buy stock in a British corporation. Does $NX = NCO$ in this case? Explain. What kind of foreign investment is this? _____

_____

_____

_____

d. Suppose the Canadian manufacturer uses the pounds to buy computer chips manufactured in Great Britain. Does $NX = NCO$ in this case? Explain.

_____

_____

3. Suppose the nominal exchange rate is 100 yen per dollar. Further, suppose the price of a baseball glove in Canada is $50 and the price of a baseball glove in Japan is 7500 yen.

a. What is the real exchange rate between Japan and Canada in terms of baseball gloves? _____

_____

_____

_____

b. Is there a profit opportunity that could be exploited with arbitrage? Where would the buying take place and where would the selling take place?

_____

c. If the nominal exchange rate stayed the same, what should happen to the price of baseball gloves in Canada and Japan? Explain. _____

_____

_____

d. Suppose prices move. What has happened to the real exchange rate?

_____

_____

4. Suppose the price of Canadian-bottled spring water is $40 per case in Canada and 600 pesos in Mexico.

a. What is the nominal peso-per-dollar exchange rate if purchasing-power parity holds? _____

b. Suppose Mexico's central bank is politically pressured to double its money supply, which in turn doubles the level of its prices. If purchasing-power parity holds, what is the new peso-per-dollar exchange rate? Did the peso appreciate or depreciate? _____

c. Suppose the Bank of Canada now doubles the Canadian money supply, which in turn doubles the level of Canadian prices. If purchasing-power parity holds, what is the value of the peso per dollar exchange rate? Did the dollar appreciate or depreciate? _____

_____

d. Compare your answers to part (a) and part (c). What has happened to the exchange rate? Why? _____

_____

_____

E. Advanced Critical Thinking

Daniel is watching a national news broadcast with his parents. The news anchor explains that the exchange rate for the Canadian dollar just hit its highest value in five years. The on-the-spot report shifts to a spokesperson for BlackBerry, a Canadian smart phone manufacturer. The spokesperson reports that foreign sales of BlackBerry's products have fallen sharply. Daniels' parents are shocked by the report's negative view of the high value of the dollar. They just booked their European vacation because of the dollar's high value.

1. Why do BlackBerry and Daniel's parents have different opinions about the value of the dollar? _____

_____

_____

_____

_____

2. BlackBerry imports many parts for its manufacturing processes and it sells many finished products abroad. Because it is upset about a high dollar, what must be true about the amounts of BlackBerry's imports and exports? _____

_____

_____

_____

_____

_____

_____

3. If someone argues that a strong dollar is "good for Canada" because Canadians are able to exchange some of their GDP for a greater amount of foreign GDP, is it true that a strong dollar is good for every Canadian? Why or why not?

_____

_____

_____

_____

_____

III. Solutions

A. True/False Questions

1. F; net exports are exports minus imports.
2. T
3. T
4. T
5. T
6. F; if exports exceed imports, the country has a trade surplus.
7. T
8. F; the exchange rate should be 150 yen per dollar.
9. T
10. F; the value of the peso should fall relative to the yen.
11. F; the real exchange rate is 1.5 German Big Macs per 1 Canadian Big Mac.
12. T
13. T
14. T
15. F; the Euro countries can have only one monetary policy.

B. Multiple-Choice Questions

1. d	5. c	9. d	13. c	17. c
2. c	6. d	10. d	14. d	18. b
3. a	7. b	11. b	15. a	19. c
4. d	8. b	12. d	16. a	20. a

C. Short-Answer Questions

1. Improved transportation, advances in telecommunications, more valuable technologically advanced products, favourable government trade policies.

2. Purchase of foreign assets by domestic residents minus purchase of domestic assets by foreigners. *NCO* decreases.

3. Domestically (*I*) or foreign countries (*NCO*) because $S = I + NCO$.

4. Domestic investment grows because less national saving is allocated abroad, and/or more foreign saving is allocated here.

5. Net exports plus the net inflow of interest and dividend payments. The current account balance decreases.

6. If Canadian prices fall, or the foreign currency-per-dollar exchange rate falls, or the foreign price level rises, then Canadian goods are less expensive to foreigners.

7.   CDN$1.11 = U.S.$1.00

8.   The first reason is that many goods are not easily traded (e.g., haircuts). The second reason is that tradable goods are not perfect substitutes (e.g., German beer versus Canadian beer).

9.   It should rise because, in the long run, a higher rate of growth of money causes a higher rate of growth in prices. Lower inflation in Canada increases the relative value of its currency.

10. Because of higher default risk or higher tax rates in Canada.

D. Practice Problems

1. a. *NCO* rises. Foreign portfolio investment.

    b. Canadian *NX* falls and a Japanese manufacturer is holding Canadian dollars, therefore *NCO* falls. Foreign portfolio investment.

    c. *NCO* falls. Foreign direct investment.

    d. *NCO* falls. Foreign portfolio investment.

    e. *NCO* rises. Foreign direct investment.

2. a. Yes, *NX* has risen by the size of the sale, and *NCO* has risen an equal amount and is the size of the company's holdings of foreign currency.

    b. Yes, *NX* has risen by the size of the sale, and *NCO* has risen an equal amount and is the size of the company's purchase of foreign capital. Foreign direct investment.

    c. Yes, *NX* has risen by the size of the sale, and *NCO* has risen an equal amount and is the size of the company's purchase of foreign capital. Foreign portfolio investment.

    d. Yes, *NX* and *NCO* are both unchanged because exports rise by the same amount as imports, leaving *NX* unchanged. *NCO* was not involved.

3. a. $\dfrac{100 \text{ yen/dollar} \times \$50 \text{ per Canadian baseball glove}}{7500 \text{ yen per Japanese baseball glove}}$

        = 0.67 Japanese baseball gloves per Canadian baseball glove

    b. Yes. Buy baseball gloves in Canada and sell them in Japan.

   c. The price should rise in Canada due to an increase in demand, and the price should fall in Japan due to an increase in supply.

   d. The real exchange rate will rise until it is equal to one (1 Japanese baseball glove to 1 Canadian baseball glove).

4. a. 600 pesos per 40 dollars = 15 pesos per dollar

   b. 1200 pesos per 40 dollars = 30 pesos per dollar; depreciate

   c. 1200 pesos per 80 dollars = 15 pesos per dollar; depreciate

   d. It is unchanged. When prices rise proportionally, it has no effect on the nominal exchange rate if purchasing-power parity holds.

E. Advanced Critical Thinking

1. BlackBerry sells many of its products to foreigners, and the high value of the Canadian dollar makes BlackBerry's products more expensive to foreigners. Daniel's parents are going to buy foreign goods and services, and the cost in Canadian dollars of those products has become lower.

2. BlackBerry must sell a greater amount of products abroad than they purchase from abroad; that is, it is a net exporter.

3. No. A strong dollar benefits Canadians who are net importers and harms Canadians who are net exporters.

13 A Macroeconomic Theory of the Small Open Economy

I. Chapter Overview

A. Context and Purpose

Chapter 13 is the second chapter in a two-chapter sequence on open-economy macroeconomics. Chapter 12 explained the basic concepts and vocabulary associated with an open economy; Chapter 13 ties these concepts together into a theory of the small open economy.

The purpose of Chapter 13 is to establish the interdependence of a number of economic variables in a small open economy. In particular, Chapter 13 demonstrates the relationships between the prices and quantities in the market for loanable funds, and the prices and quantities in the market for foreign-currency exchange. Using these markets, one can analyze the impact of a variety of economic events and government policies on an economy's exchange rate and trade balance.

B. Helpful Hints

1. *A change in national saving generates the same results, regardless of whether the change was from private saving or public saving.* In the text, there is a demonstration of the impact of an increase in a government budget deficit on a small open economy. It is shown that an increase in a budget deficit causes a reduction in the public saving component of national saving that shifts the supply of loanable funds to the left. However, a reduction in the private saving component of national saving would also shift the supply of loanable funds to the left. Thus, the example given in the text can be utilized for cases when there is a change in private saving.

2. *To find the change in* NX *(net exports), remember that* NX = NCO *(net capital outflow).* When the model is used to discover the impact of a government policy or an economic event on the economic variables in an open economy, there is no way to directly read net exports (the trade balance) from any of the graphs. However, the quantity of *NCO* is always directly measurable as the supply of dollars in the market for foreign-currency exchange. Because *NCO = NX*, whenever there is an increase in *NCO*, there is an equivalent increase in *NX* (which is an improvement in the trade balance). Whenever *NCO* declines, there is an equivalent decline in *NX*.

3. *Capital flight reduces domestic investment.* The discussion of capital flight in the text notes that capital flight increases net capital outflow and the supply of the domestic currency on the foreign-currency exchange market, which then lowers the exchange value of the domestic currency. Since these activities raise net exports (improve the trade balance), why is capital flight considered bad for the economy rather than good? Look at panel (a) of Figure 13.7 in the text. Because borrowers must now pay a higher interest rate than they paid before the crisis of confidence, the quantity of loanable funds demanded for domestic investment falls. Domestic investment is reduced by an amount equal to the increase in net exports. Capital flight, therefore, reduces domestic investment and, with it, the prospect for long-term economic growth in the country.

4. *Work the examples in the text backward.* The examples demonstrated in your text require a significant degree of concentration to understand. Once you have mastered them, you should feel comfortable that you can follow someone else's demonstration. The next step is to work those same examples backward, alone. (See Practice Problem #1.) That is, address the effect of a decrease in the world interest rate, a reduction in the budget deficit, the lowering of a trade restriction, and the effect of capital inflow.

II. Self-Testing Challenge

A. True/False Questions

_____1.   Net capital outflow is the purchase of domestic assets by foreigners minus the purchase of foreign assets by domestic residents.

_____2.   A country's net capital outflow (*NCO*) is always equal to its net exports (*NX*).

_____3.   Other things being the same, an increase in the world real interest rate increases net capital outflow for a small open economy.

_____4.   An increase in Canadian net capital outflow increases the supply of dollars in the market for foreign-currency exchange and decreases the real exchange rate of the dollar.

_____5.   If labour unions convince Canadians to "buy Canadian," it will improve the Canadian trade balance.

_____6.   Net capital outflow is negative when domestic investment exceeds national saving at the world interest rate.

_____7.   An increase in the government's budget deficit shifts the supply of loanable funds to the right.

_____8.   An increase in the government's budget deficit tends to cause the real exchange rate of the dollar to depreciate.

_____9.   The fall in government budget deficits over the 1995–2007 period reduced net exports.

_____10.   If Canada raises its tariff on imported wine, it will reduce imports and improve the trade balance.

_____11.   If Canada raises its tariff on imported wine, domestic wine producers will benefit, but the dollar will appreciate and domestic producers of export goods will be harmed.

_____12.   An increase in the government budget surplus causes the real exchange rate to depreciate.

_____13.   In 2012, Greece was experiencing capital flight as citizens withdrew their savings from Greek banks and moved the money abroad.

_____14.   If Canadians increase their saving, the dollar will appreciate in the market for foreign-currency exchange.

_____15.   The trilemma in international finance is that a country can only achieve two of the following: free capital mobility, a national monetary policy, and a stable exchange rate.

B. Multiple-Choice Questions

1. Which one of the following statements regarding the loanable funds market in a small open economy is **NOT** true?
    a. The real interest rate is equal to the world real interest rate.
    b. Net capital outflow is positive when the demand for loanable funds exceeds the supply of loanable funds at the world interest rate.
    c. Domestic investment determines the demand for loanable funds.
    d. National saving determines the supply of loanable funds.

2. Which one of the following is an outcome of an increase in the government budget deficit?
    a. It increases net exports.
    b. It reduces net capital outflow.
    c. It increases the demand for loanable funds.
    d. It causes the real exchange rate to depreciate.

3. Which one of the following statements regarding the loanable funds market is true?
    a. An increase in private saving shifts the supply of loanable funds to the left.
    b. A decrease in the government budget surplus increases national saving.
    c. An increase in the government budget surplus shifts the supply of loanable funds to the right.
    d. An increase in the government budget surplus shifts the supply of loanable funds to the left.

4. Which one of the following is an outcome of a higher world real interest rate, assuming other things are equal?
    a. It causes the Canadian dollar to appreciate.
    b. It increases Canadian net capital outflow.
    c. It increases the quantity demanded of loanable funds for domestic investment.
    d. It decreases the quantity supplied of loanable funds from national saving.

5. Which one of the following would be an outcome if Europe's taste for Canadian-produced wine increased?
    a. The dollar would depreciate and Canadian net exports would increase.
    b. The dollar would depreciate and Canadian net exports would decrease.
    c. The dollar would appreciate and Canadian net exports would increase.
    d. The dollar would appreciate but Canadian net exports would stay the same.

6. Which one of the following is an outcome of a decrease in the federal government budget deficit?
    a. Canadian net exports would increase and Canadian net capital outflow would decrease.
    b. Canadian net exports would decrease and Canadian net capital outflow would increase.
    c. Canadian net exports and Canadian net capital outflow would decrease by the same amount.
    d. Canadian net exports and Canadian net capital outflow would increase by the same amount.

7. Which one of the following is the result of an increase in a government budget surplus?
    a. an increase in domestic investment
    b. a decrease in domestic investment
    c. an increase in net exports
    d. a decrease in net exports

8. Which one of the following statements regarding the market for foreign-currency exchange is true?
   a. An increase in Canadian net exports increases the supply of dollars and the dollar depreciates.
   b. An increase in Canadian net exports decreases the supply of dollars and the dollar depreciates.
   c. An increase in Canadian net exports decreases the demand for dollars and the dollar appreciates.
   d. An increase in Canadian net exports increases the demand for dollars and the dollar appreciates.

9. Which one of the following statements regarding the market for foreign-currency exchange is true?
   a. An increase in Canadian net capital outflow increases the supply of dollars and the dollar appreciates.
   b. An increase in Canadian net capital outflow increases the supply of dollars and the dollar depreciates.
   c. An increase in Canadian net capital outflow increases the demand for dollars and the dollar appreciates.
   d. An increase in Canadian net capital outflow increases the demand for dollars and the dollar depreciates.

10. If Canada imposes a quota on the importing of apparel produced in China, which one of the following is true regarding the market for foreign-currency exchange?
    a. The supply of dollars increases and the dollar depreciates.
    b. The supply of dollars decreases and the dollar appreciates.
    c. The demand for dollars increases and the dollar appreciates.
    d. The demand for dollars decreases and the dollar depreciates.

11. If Canada imposes a quota on the importing of apparel produced in China, which one of the following is true regarding Canadian net exports?
    a. Net exports will rise.
    b. Net exports will fall.
    c. Net exports will remain unchanged.

12. Suppose, due to political instability, Mexicans suddenly choose to invest in Canadian assets as opposed to Mexican assets. Which one of the following statements is true regarding Canadian net capital outflow?
    a. Canadian net capital outflow rises.
    b. Canadian net capital outflow falls.
    c. Canadian net capital outflow is unchanged because only Canadian residents can alter Canadian net capital outflow.

13. Suppose, due to political instability, Mexicans suddenly choose to invest in Canadian assets as opposed to Mexican assets. Which one of the following statements is true regarding the value of the dollar and Canadian net exports?
    a. The dollar appreciates and Canadian net exports fall.
    b. The dollar depreciates and Canadian net exports fall.
    c. The dollar appreciates and Canadian net exports rise.
    d. The dollar depreciates and Canadian net exports rise.

14. Which one of the following is an outcome of an increase in Canadian private saving?
    a. Canadian net exports increase and Canadian net capital outflow decreases.
    b. Canadian net exports decrease and Canadian net capital outflow increases.
    c. Canadian net exports and Canadian net capital outflow decrease by the same amount.
    d. Canadian net exports and Canadian net capital outflow increase by the same amount.

15. Which one of the following statements about trade policy is true?
    a. A restrictive import quota increases a country's net exports.
    b. A restrictive import quota decreases a country's net exports.
    c. A country's trade policy has no impact on the size of its trade balance.

16. Which one of the following groups would **NOT** benefit from a Canadian import quota on Japanese autos?
    a. Canadian farmers who export grain
    b. shareholders (owners) of Canadian auto manufacturers
    c. members of the Canadian Auto Workers' union
    d. Canadian consumers who buy electronics from Japan

17. Which one of the following is an example of a trade policy?
    a. a tariff on footwear
    b. capital flight, because it increases a country's net exports
    c. an increase in the government budget deficit, because it reduces a country's net exports
    d. an increase in the world interest rate, because it increases a country's net exports

18. Which one of the following should have the same effect on the exchange rate as an export subsidy?
    a. a tariff
    b. capital flight
    c. an increase in private saving
    d. an increase in the government budget surplus

19. Which one of the following groups would be **MOST** harmed by a Canadian government budget deficit?
    a. borrowers of loanable funds
    b. Canadians who wish to travel abroad
    c. a Canadian winery selling wine to the United States
    d. Canadian residents wishing to buy foreign-produced autos

20. Which of the following best explains the effects of capital flight?
    a. It decreases a country's net exports and increases its long-run growth path.
    b. It decreases a country's net exports and decreases its long-run growth path.
    c. It increases a country's net exports and decreases its long-run growth path.
    d. It increases a country's net exports and increases its long-run growth path.

C. Short-Answer Questions

1. How is net capital outflow determined in a small open economy with perfect capital mobility? _____

2. Explain the source of the supply of dollars in the market for foreign-currency exchange. _____

3. Explain the source of the demand for dollars in the market for foreign-currency exchange. _____

4. Why might certain companies and unions support tariffs and import quotas even if they know that these restrictions cannot alter the trade balance? _____

5. Suppose the quality of Canadian goods and services falls and, as a result, foreigners choose to buy fewer Canadian goods. Does this affect the Canadian balance of trade? Why or why not? _____

6. What happens to the value of a country's currency if there is capital flight from that country? Explain. _____

7. What would an increase in the saving of Canadian residents do to the Canadian trade balance and the dollar exchange rate? Explain. _____

    _____

    _____

8. Why are budget deficits and trade deficits related to each other? _____

    _____

    _____

9. In Canada, we have free capital mobility and a national monetary policy. In the fundamental trilemma of international finance, what goal must Canada give up?

    _____

D. Practice Problems

1. This problem is composed from the examples in the chapter, except that the source of the change has been reversed. Use the model in the textbook to answer the following questions.

    a. Suppose there is a decrease in the world interest rate. Describe the sequence of events in the model by describing the shifts in the curves, and discuss the movements in the relevant macroeconomic variables. _____

        _____

        _____

        _____

        _____

        _____

    b. Suppose the government reduces its budget deficit. Describe the sequence of events in the model by describing the shifts in the curves, and discuss the movements in the relevant macroeconomic variables. _____

        _____

        _____

        _____

        _____

        _____

    c. Suppose the government removes a quota on the importing of Japanese automobiles. Describe the sequence of events in the model by describing the shifts in the curves, and discuss the movements in the relevant macroeconomic variables._____

        _____

        _____

        _____

        _____

        _____

d. Suppose the perceived risk of holding Mexican assets disappears, and borrowers in Mexico can pay the world interest rate. Describe the sequence of events in the model by describing the shifts in the curves, and discuss the movements in the relevant macroeconomic variables. _____

_____

_____

_____

_____

_____

_____

2. a. Suppose private saving increased at each real interest rate. What would happen to the important macroeconomic variables in our model of an open economy? _____

_____

_____

_____

b. Is there any difference between the answer above and the answer one would write if the government had increased its budget surplus? Why or why not?

_____

_____

c. Suppose the government passes an investment tax credit that increases domestic investment at each real interest rate. How would this change the important economic variables in the model? _____

_____

_____

_____

d. Compare the answer in part (a) (an increase in saving at each real interest rate) to the answer in part (c) (an increase in domestic investment at each real interest rate). Are there any differences? _____

_____

_____

3. Suppose Canadian preferences for Swiss chocolates increase. Answer these questions using the open-economy model from the perspective of Switzerland.

a. What happens to the demand for Swiss francs in the foreign-currency exchange market? _____

_____

b. What happens to the value of the Swiss franc in the foreign-currency exchange market? _____

_____

c. What happens to Switzerland's net exports? Why? _____

_____

d. If Switzerland is exporting more chocolate, what must be true about Swiss imports and exports of other items? _____

_____

_____

_____

e. Keeping in mind your answers to parts (a) through (d), do you think that Switzerland's trade balance with the rest of the world is based on the superior quality of its chocolates? Explain. _____

_____

_____

_____

4. Suppose Canada is perceived to be politically unstable and this induces capital flight to the United States.

a. Describe what happens in the foreign-currency exchange market from the perspective of Canada. _____

_____

_____

b. Describe what happens in the foreign-currency exchange market from the perspective of the United States. _____

_____

c. Are the answers to parts (a) and (b) above consistent with one another? Why or why not? _____

_____

_____

_____

d. What should this event do to each country's balance of trade?

_____

_____

e. Which country will tend to grow faster in the future? Why? _____

_____

_____

_____

E. Advanced Critical Thinking

Hong Kong has a capitalist economic system. It was leased from China by Great Britain for 100 years. In 1997, it was returned to China, which was at that time a socialist republic.

1. What do you think happened to the net capital outflow of Hong Kong from 1990 to 1997? Why? _____

    _____

    _____

    _____

2. The residents of Hong Kong chose Canada, particularly the Vancouver area, as a place to move some of their business activity. What impact do you suppose this had on Canada's net capital outflow, net exports, and exchange rate?

    _____

    _____

    _____

3. Which Canadian industries, those engaged in importing or exporting, would likely have been pleased with Hong Kong's investment in Canada? Why?

    _____

    _____

    _____

4. What impact did Hong Kong's return to China have on the long-term economic growth rate of Canada? _____

    _____

    _____

III. Solutions

A. True/False Questions

1. F; *NCO* is the purchase of foreign assets by domestic residents minus the purchase of domestic assets by foreigners.
2. T
3. T
4. T
5. F; net exports are unchanged because *NCO* is unchanged.
6. T
7. F; an increase in the government's budget deficit shifts the supply of loanable funds to the left.
8. F; an increase in the government's budget deficit raises the real exchange rate.
9. F; a decrease in budget deficits causes the dollar to depreciate and causes net exports to rise.

10. F; net exports are unchanged because *NCO* is unchanged.
11. T
12. T
13. T
14. F; the dollar will depreciate.
15. T

B. Multiple-Choice Questions

1. b	5. d	9. b	13. a	17. a
2. b	6. d	10. c	14. d	18. a
3. c	7. c	11. c	15. c	19. c
4. b	8. d	12. b	16. a	20. c

C. Short-Answer Questions

1. *NCO* is determined by the difference between the supply of loanable funds (national saving) and the demand for loanable funds (domestic investment) at the world interest rate.

2. It comes from dollars that Canadians use for *NCO*.

3. It comes from the need for dollars from foreigners purchasing Canadian *NX*.

4. Trade restrictions can improve the sales of some domestic companies facing competition from imports, but largely at the expense of other domestic companies producing for export.

5. No. It reduces the demand for dollars in the market for foreign-currency exchange and lowers the value of the dollar to keep *NX* unchanged.

6. It increases the supply of the country's currency in the market for foreign-currency exchange and lowers the exchange rate.

7. It increases *NCO*, increases the supply of dollars on the foreign-currency exchange market, lowers the dollar exchange rate, and increases *NX*.

8. A budget deficit reduces national saving, net capital outflow, and net exports.

9. Stability in the foreign exchange rate of its currency.

D. Practice Problems

1. a. A decrease in the world interest rate reduces the quantity supplied of loanable funds and increases the quantity demanded of loanable funds. As a result, net capital outflow decreases, which in turn shifts the supply-of-dollars curve in the foreign exchange market to the left. The real exchange rate appreciates, causing net exports to fall.

    b. A decrease in the government budget deficit increases national saving, which shifts the supply-of-loanable-funds curve to the right. Net capital outflow increases, which in turn shifts the supply-of-dollars curve in the foreign exchange market to the right. The real exchange rate depreciates, causing net exports to rise.

    c. The removal of an import quota has no impact in the market for loanable funds. Net capital outflow is not affected; therefore, the supply-of-dollars curve in the foreign exchange market does not shift. The demand-for-dollars curve shifts to the left, causing the real exchange rate to depreciate. There is no change in the trade balance, but there is a higher volume of trade (more imports and more exports).

    d. With no risk premium, the interest rate paid on Mexican assets is the world interest rate. The supply-of-loanable-funds curve shifts down, leaving the quantity supplied of loanable funds unchanged. The quantity demanded of loanable funds increases, resulting in a fall in net capital outflow. The supply-of-pesos curve in the foreign exchange market shifts to the left, which causes the peso to appreciate and net exports to fall.

2. a. The supply of loanable funds shifts right, *NCO* increases, thus increasing the supply of dollars in the foreign-currency exchange market, which causes the real exchange rate to depreciate and net exports to rise.

    b. No, because it does not matter why national saving increased. Either one will shift the supply of loanable funds to the right.

    c. It would increase in the demand for loanable funds, lower *NCO*, and decrease the supply of dollars in the foreign-currency exchange market, which would cause the real exchange rate to appreciate and net exports to fall.

    d. An increase in saving moves the trade balance toward surplus, while an increase in investment demand moves the trade balance toward deficit.

3. a. shifts right

    b. Real exchange rate rises and therefore the value of the Swiss franc rises.

    c. *NCO* is unchanged; therefore, *NX* as a total is unchanged.

    d. If *NX* is constant, Switzerland must be importing more or exporting less of other items.

    e. *NX* as a total are determined by *NCO*, so Switzerland's overall trade balance is based on its national saving and domestic investment. However, the composition of its exports may be based on its relative quality of production.

4. a. The supply of Canadian dollars shifts right, and the value of the Canadian dollar falls.

    b. The supply of U.S. dollars shifts left, and the value of the U.S. dollar rises.

    c. Yes. A rise in the value of the U.S. dollar relative to the Canadian dollar should correspond to the fall in the value of the Canadian dollar relative to the U.S. dollar.

    d. The fall in the value of the Canadian dollar will improve Canada's *NX*, while the stronger U.S. dollar will lower *NX* by the United States.

    e. Canada is increasing its *NCO* to the United States and the United States is decreasing its *NCO* to Canada; therefore, the United States will likely grow faster.

E. Advanced Critical Thinking

1. The *NCO* of Hong Kong increased because foreigners were not buying assets in Hong Kong and Hong Kong residents were buying assets abroad—capital flight. Investors feared that China would nationalize much of Hong Kong's industry.

2. This decreased Canada's *NCO*. A reduced *NCO* reduces the supply of Canadian dollars in the foreign-currency exchange market, raises the exchange rate, and lowers net exports.

3. The increase in the value of the Canadian dollar made Canadian producers less competitive abroad, but made Canadian imports cheaper. Thus, exporters were hurt, while companies that import were better off.

4. The reduction in Canada's *NCO* (due to Hong Kong's increased *NCO*) increased the capital stock of Canada, thus causing faster economic growth.

CHAPTER 14 Aggregate Demand and Aggregate Supply

I. Chapter Overview

A. Context and Purpose

To this point, our study of macroeconomic theory has concentrated on the behaviour of the economy in the long run. Chapters 14–16 now focus on short-run fluctuations in the economy around its long-run trend. Chapter 14 introduces aggregate demand and aggregate supply, and shows how shifts in these curves can cause recessions. Chapter 15 focuses on how policymakers use the tools of monetary and fiscal policy to influence aggregate demand. Chapter 16 addresses the short-run relationship between inflation and unemployment.

The purpose of Chapter 14 is to develop the model that economists use to analyze the economy's short-run fluctuations: the model of aggregate demand and aggregate supply. The sources for shifts in the aggregate-demand curve and the aggregate-supply curve are discussed and how these shifts can cause recessions. Chapter 14 also introduces the actions policymakers might undertake to offset recessions.

B. Helpful Hints

1. *There are no changes in real variables along the long-run aggregate-supply curve.* When all prices change equally, no real variables have changed. A vertical long-run aggregate-supply curve demonstrates this classic lesson. Pick any point on the long-run aggregate-supply curve. Now double the price level and all nominal values, such as wages. Although the price level has doubled, relative prices have remained constant, including the real wage. There has been no change in anyone's incentive to produce, and thus no change in output. It follows that if the economy is temporarily producing a level of output other than the long-run natural rate of output, then at least some wages or prices have failed to adjust to the long-run equilibrium price level, which causes at least some relative prices to change so as to stimulate or discourage production. This is, in fact, what is happening along a short-run aggregate-supply curve.

2. *Output can fluctuate to levels both above and below the natural rate of output.* The examples of economic fluctuations in the text focus on recessions. That is, the examples deal with periods when output is less than the natural rate of output. Note, however, that output can be above the natural rate of output temporarily because unemployment can be below the natural rate of unemployment. This will occur when there is a positive aggregate demand shock—for example, if there is an increase in exports or an increase in domestic investment. It will also occur if there is a positive aggregate supply shock—for example, if the price of oil were to

fall or if union wage demands were to decrease. These cases are addressed in the problems that follow.

3. *Tables 14.1 and 14.2 in the textbook provide a very useful summary of the aggregate-demand and aggregate-supply curves.* The textbook explains that an increase in the expected price level shifts the short-run aggregate-supply curve to the left. It is helpful to remember that such shifts often are caused by increases in production costs, such as higher nominal wages or higher natural resource prices.

II. Self-Testing Challenges

When necessary, draw a graph of the model of aggregate demand and aggregate supply on scratch paper to help determine the answers to the following problems and questions.

A. True/False Questions

_____1.   Over the past century, Canadian real GDP per person has grown, on average, at about 2 percent per year.

_____2.   Investment is a particularly volatile component of spending across the business cycle.

_____3.   When real GDP declines, the unemployment rate also declines.

_____4.   If the classical dichotomy and monetary neutrality hold in the long run, then the long-run aggregate-supply curve should be vertical.

_____5.   Economists refer to fluctuations in output as the "business cycle" because movements in output are regular and predictable.

_____6.   One reason aggregate demand slopes downward is the wealth effect: A decrease in the price level increases the real value of money holdings, and consumer spending rises.

_____7.   If the Bank of Canada increases the money supply, the aggregate-demand curve shifts to the left.

_____8.   A social recession happens when individuals, families, and communities are affected by financial loss, fear, and declining physical and mental health.

_____9.   A rise in price expectations that causes wages to rise causes the short-run aggregate-supply curve to shift left.

_____10.   If the economy is in a recession, the economy will adjust to long-run equilibrium on its own as wages and price expectations rise.

____11.   In the short run, if the government cuts back spending significantly to balance its budget, a recession may result.

____12.   The short-run effect of an increase in short-run aggregate supply is an increase in output and an increase in the price level.

____13.   A sharp rise in the price of oil can cause stagflation.

____14.   Monetary policy and fiscal policy actions during 2008–2009 helped minimize the severity of the recession.

____15.   If policymakers choose to try to move the economy out of a recession, they should use their policy tools to decrease aggregate demand.

B. Multiple-Choice Questions

1.   Which one of the following statements about economic fluctuations is true?
   a.   A depression is a mild recession.
   b.   A recession is when output rises above the natural rate of output.
   c.   Economic fluctuations have been termed the "business cycle" because the movements in output are regular and predictable.
   d.   A variety of spending, income, and output measures can be used to measure economic fluctuations because most macroeconomic quantities tend to fluctuate together.

2.   Which one of the following would shift the aggregate-demand curve to the left?
   a.   a fall in interest rates
   b.   a rise in personal income taxes
   c.   an exchange rate depreciation
   d.   an increase in government spending on highways

3.   Which one of the following would shift the aggregate-demand curve for Canada to the right?
   a.   a fall in expected future profits by firms
   b.   a decrease in the money supply
   c.   a boom in the stock market
   d.   a recession in the United States

4.   Which one of the following is **NOT** a reason why the aggregate-demand curve slopes downward?
   a.   the wealth effect
   b.   the interest-rate effect
   c.   the real exchange-rate effect
   d.   the classical dichotomy/monetary neutrality effects

5. In the model of aggregate supply and aggregate demand, which one of the following is the initial impact of an increase in consumer optimism?
    a. a shift of aggregate demand to the left
    b. a shift of aggregate demand to the right
    c. a shift of short-run aggregate supply to the left
    d. a shift of short-run aggregate supply to the right

6. Which one of the following statements describes what occurs in a long-run aggregate-supply curve?
    a. The long-run aggregate-supply curve shifts left when the natural rate of unemployment falls.
    b. The long-run aggregate-supply curve shifts right when the government raises the minimum wage.
    c. The long-run aggregate-supply curve is vertical because an equal change in all prices and wages leaves output unaffected.
    d. The long-run aggregate-supply curve is positively sloped because price expectations and wages tend to be fixed in the long run.

7. Which one of the following is a reason that the aggregate-demand curve slopes downward (negatively), according to the wealth effect?
    a. Lower prices increase the real value of money holdings, and consumer spending increases.
    b. Lower prices decrease the real value of money holdings, and consumer spending decreases.
    c. Lower prices reduce money holdings and increase lending, interest rates fall, and investment spending increases.
    d. Lower prices increase money holdings and decrease lending, interest rates rise, and investment spending falls.

8. Which one of the following is the natural rate of output?
    a. The amount of real GDP produced when there is no unemployment.
    b. The amount of real GDP produced when the economy is at the natural rate of investment.
    c. The amount of real GDP produced when the economy is at the natural rate of aggregate demand.
    d. The amount of real GDP produced when the economy is at the natural rate of unemployment.

9. Which one of the following refers to a scenario in which the price level falls, but because of fixed nominal wage contracts, the real wage rises and firms cut back on production?
    a. the misperceptions theory of the short-run aggregate-supply curve
    b. the sticky-wage theory of the short-run aggregate-supply curve
    c. the sticky-price theory of the short-run aggregate-supply curve
    d. the classical dichotomy theory of the short-run aggregate-supply curve

10. Suppose the price level falls but suppliers notice only that the price of their particular product has fallen. Thinking there has been a fall in the relative price of their product, they cut back on production. Which one of the following refers to this scenario?
   a. the misperceptions theory of the short-run aggregate-supply curve
   b. the sticky-wage theory of the short-run aggregate-supply curve
   c. the sticky-price theory of the short-run aggregate-supply curve
   d. the classical dichotomy theory of the short-run aggregate-supply curve

11. Suppose the economy is initially in long-run equilibrium. Then suppose there is a reduction in investment spending by firms. According to the model of aggregate demand and aggregate supply, which one of the following is what happens to prices and output in the *short run*?
   a. prices rise, output rises
   b. prices rise, output falls
   c. prices fall, output falls
   d. prices fall, output rises

12. Suppose the economy is initially in long-run equilibrium. Then suppose there is a reduction in investment spending by firms. If the policymakers allow the economy to adjust to long-run equilibrium on its own, according to the model of aggregate demand and aggregate supply, which one of the following is what happens to prices and output in the *long run*?
   a. prices rise, output is unchanged from its initial value
   b. prices fall, output is unchanged from its initial value
   c. output rises, prices are unchanged from the initial value
   d. output falls, prices are unchanged from the initial value

13. Suppose the economy is initially in long-run equilibrium. Then suppose there is a drought that destroys much of the wheat crop. According to the model of aggregate demand and aggregate supply, which one of the following is what happens to prices and output in the *short run*?
   a. prices rise, output rises
   b. prices rise, output falls
   c. prices fall, output falls
   d. prices fall, output rises

14. Suppose the economy is initially in long-run equilibrium. Then suppose there is a drought that destroys much of the wheat crop. If the policymakers allow the economy to adjust to long-run equilibrium on its own, according to the model of aggregate demand and aggregate supply, what happens to prices and output in the *long run*?
   a. prices rise, output is unchanged from its initial value
   b. prices fall, output is unchanged from its initial value
   c. output rises, prices are unchanged from the initial value
   d. output and price level are unchanged from their initial values

15. Which one of the following describes when stagflation occurs?
    a. when there are falling prices and falling output
    b. when there are falling prices and rising output
    c. when there are rising prices and rising output
    d. when there are rising prices and falling output

16. Which one of the following events leads to an initial impact that takes the form of a shift in the short-run aggregate-supply curve to the right?
    a. a drop in oil prices
    b. a decrease in the money supply
    c. an increase in price expectations
    d. an increase in government spending on military equipment

17. Suppose the economy is operating in a recession. If policymakers wished to move output to its long-run natural rate, which one of the following should they attempt to do?
    a. Shift aggregate demand to the right.
    b. Shift aggregate demand to the left.
    c. Shift short-run aggregate supply to the right.
    d. Shift short-run aggregate supply to the left.

18. Suppose the economy is operating in a recession. If policymakers allow the economy to adjust to the long-run natural rate on its own, which one of the following describes the likely outcome?
    a. People will raise their price expectations and aggregate demand will shift left.
    b. People will reduce their price expectations and aggregate demand will shift right.
    c. People will raise their price expectations and the short-run aggregate supply will shift left.
    d. People will reduce their price expectations and the short-run aggregate supply will shift right.

19. According to the model of aggregate supply and aggregate demand, in the long run, which one of the following describes the effects of an increase in the money supply?
    a. It should cause prices to rise and output to rise.
    b. It should cause prices to fall and output to fall.
    c. It should cause prices to rise and output to remain unchanged.
    d. It should cause prices to fall and output to remain unchanged.

20. Which one of the following actions by policymakers is said to "accommodate" an adverse supply shock?
    a. respond to the adverse supply shock by decreasing short-run aggregate supply
    b. fail to respond to the adverse supply shock and allow the economy to adjust on its own
    c. respond to the adverse supply shock by increasing aggregate demand, which further raises prices
    d. respond to the adverse supply shock by decreasing aggregate demand, which lowers prices

C. Short-Answer Questions

1. Name the three key facts about economic fluctuations. _____
   _____
   _____

2. Which component of aggregate demand varies the **MOST** over the business cycle? _____
   _____
   _____

3. What happens to the natural rate of output when the natural rate of unemployment falls? _____
   _____
   _____

4. What are the three reasons the aggregate-demand curve slopes downward? Explain them. _____
   _____
   _____
   _____
   _____
   _____

5. Suppose the economy is in long-run equilibrium. If the sticky-wage theory of the short-run aggregate-supply curve is employed, what initially happens to the real wage if there is a decrease in aggregate demand? _____
   _____
   _____

6. Referring to question 5, if the economy is to adjust on its own back to the long-run equilibrium level of output, what must happen to the real wage?
   _____
   _____
   _____

7. If the economy is in a recession, why might policymakers choose to adjust aggregate demand to eliminate the recession rather than let the economy adjust— or self-correct—on its own? _____
_____
_____
_____

8. Does a shift in aggregate demand alter output in the long run? Why or why not?
_____
_____
_____

9. Why is a decrease in the money supply unlikely to be neutral in the short run?
_____
_____
_____
_____

10. How did the model of short-run economic fluctuations develop?
_____
_____
_____

11. What causes both the short-run and long-run aggregate-supply curves to shift together? _____
_____
_____

12. What causes only the short-run aggregate-supply curve to shift, while the long-run aggregate-supply curve remains stationary? _____
_____
_____

D. Practice Problems

1. Four cases are listed below. Trace the impact of each shock in the aggregate-supply aggregate-demand model by answering the following three questions for each case:

(i) What happens to prices and output in the short run?

(ii) What happens to prices and output in the long run if the economy is allowed to adjust to long-run equilibrium on its own?

(iii) If policymakers had intervened to move output back to the natural rate of output instead of allowing the economy to self-correct, in which direction should they have moved aggregate demand?

a. Aggregate demand shifts left. _____

_____

_____

_____

b. Aggregate demand shifts right. _____

_____

_____

_____

c. Short-run aggregate supply shifts left. _____

_____

_____

_____

d. Short-run aggregate supply shifts right. _____

_____

_____

_____

2. The following events have their *initial impact* on which one of the following: aggregate demand, long-run aggregate supply, or short-run aggregate supply? Does the curve shift to the right or left?

a. The government repairs aging roads and bridges._____

_____

b. OPEC raises oil prices. _____

_____

c. The government raises Employment Insurance benefits. _____

_____

d. Canadians feel more secure in their jobs and become more optimistic.

_____

e. A technological advance takes place in the application of computers to the production of steel. _____

_____

f. The government increases the minimum wage. _____

_____

g. Wage demands of new university graduates fall. _____

_____

h. The Bank of Canada decreases the money supply. _____
_____

i. A drought destroys much of the corn crop. _____
_____

3. Suppose the economy is in long-run equilibrium. Then suppose the Bank of Canada suddenly increases the money supply.

a. Describe the initial impact of this event in the model of aggregate demand and aggregate supply by explaining which curve shifts which way.
_____

b. What happens to the price level and real output in the short run?
_____

c. If the economy is allowed to adjust to the increase in the money supply, what happens to the price level and real output in the long run (compared to their original levels)?
_____

d. Does an increase in the money supply move output above the natural rate indefinitely? Why or why not?
_____
_____

4. Suppose the economy is in long-run equilibrium. Then suppose workers and firms suddenly expect higher prices in the future and agree to an increase in wages.

a. Describe the initial impact of this event in the model of aggregate demand and aggregate supply by explaining which curve shifts which way.
_____

b. What happens to the price level and real output in the short run?
_____

c. What name do we have for this combination of movements in output and prices? _____
_____

d. If policymakers wanted to move output back to the natural rate of output, what should they do? _____
_____

e. If policymakers were able to move output back to the natural rate of output, what would the policy do to prices? _____
_____

f. If policymakers did nothing at all, what would happen to the wage rate as the economy self-corrects, or adjusts back to the natural rate of output on its own?

_____

_____

g. Is it likely that an increase in price expectations and wages alone can cause a permanent increase in the price level? Why or why not? _____

_____

_____

5. Suppose aggregate demand has decreased and the economy is in a recession. Describe the adjustment process necessary for the economy to adjust on its own to the natural rate of output for each of the three theoretical short-run aggregate-supply curves.

a. The misperceptions theory: _____

_____

_____

_____

_____

b. The sticky-wage theory: _____

_____

_____

_____

_____

_____

c. The sticky-price theory: _____

_____

_____

_____

_____

d. Would the type of adjustments described above take place more slowly from a recession or from a period when output was above the long-run natural rate? Why? _____

_____

_____

_____

E. Advanced Critical Thinking

Jacquie is watching the evening news on television. The news anchor reports that union wage demands are much higher this year because the workers anticipate an increase in the rate of inflation. Her roommate Estelle says, "Inflation is a self-fulfilling prophecy. If workers think there will be higher prices, they demand higher wages. This increases the cost of production and firms raise their prices. Expecting higher prices simply causes higher prices."

1.   Is this true in the short run? Explain._____
    _____
    _____

2.   If policymakers do nothing and allow the economy to adjust to the natural rate of output on its own, does expecting higher prices cause higher prices in the long run? Explain. _____
    _____
    _____

3.   If policymakers accommodate the adverse supply shock, does the expectation of higher prices cause higher prices in the long run? Explain. _____
    _____
    _____

III. Solutions

A. True/False Questions

1.   T
2.   T
3.   F; as output falls, unemployment rises.
4.   T
5.   F; fluctuations in output are irregular and unpredictable.
6.   T
7.   F; aggregate demand shifts to the right.
8.   T.
9.   T
10.   F; in a recession, the economy adjusts to long-run equilibrium as wages and price expectations fall.
11.   T
12.   F; the effect is an increase in output and a decrease in the price level.
13.   T
14.   T
15.   F; policymakers should increase aggregate demand.

B. Multiple-Choice Questions

1. d	5. b	9. b	13. b	17. a
2. b	6. c	10. a	14. d	18. d
3. c	7. a	11. c	15. d	19. c
4. d	8. d	12. b	16. a	20. c

C. Short-Answer Questions

1. Economic fluctuations are irregular and unpredictable, most macroeconomic quantities fluctuate together, and when output falls, unemployment rises.

2. investment spending

3. A fall in the natural rate of unemployment would increase the natural rate of output, and shift the long-run aggregate-supply curve to the right.

4. Wealth effect: Lower prices increase the real value of money holdings, and consumer spending increases. Interest rate effect: Lower prices reduce the quantity of money held, some money is loaned, interest rates fall, and investment spending increases. Real exchange-rate effect: Lower prices decrease the real exchange rate, and net exports increase.

5. Because the nominal wage is fixed for a period, the fall in the price level raises the real wage.

6. The nominal wage must fall so that the real wage can return to its initial level.

7. They think they can get the economy back to the long-run natural rate of output more quickly, or, in the case of a negative supply shock, they are more concerned with output and employment than inflation.

8. No. In the long run, output is determined by factor supplies and technology (long-run aggregate supply). Changes in aggregate demand affect output only in the short run because relative prices are only temporarily altered.

9. A decrease in aggregate demand arising from a decrease in the money supply lowers the price level unexpectedly. Some prices and wages are sticky and adjust to the lower price level slower than others, causing a fall in output in the short run.

10. The model is a by-product of the Great Depression of the 1930s. In 1936, economist John Maynard Keynes developed the theory that recessions can occur because of inadequate aggregate demand.

11.   Changes in labour, capital, natural resources, and technology shift the short-run and long-run aggregate-supply curves together.

12.   Changes in the expected price level shift only the short-run aggregate-supply curve.

D. Practice Problems

1.   a.   Prices fall, output falls. Prices fall, output returns to the natural rate. Shift aggregate demand to the right.

b.   Prices rise, output rises. Prices rise, output returns to the natural rate. Shift aggregate demand to the left.

c.   Prices rise, output falls. Price level returns to original value, output returns to the natural rate. Shift aggregate demand to the right.

d.   Prices fall, output rises. Price level returns to original value, output returns to the natural rate. Shift aggregate demand to the left.

2.   a.   aggregate demand; right

b.   short-run aggregate supply; left

c.   short-run and long-run aggregate supply; left

d.   aggregate demand; right

e.   short-run and long-run aggregate supply; right

f.   short-run and long-run aggregate supply; left

g.   short-run aggregate supply; right

h.   aggregate demand; left

i.   short-run aggregate supply; left

3.   a.   Aggregate demand shifts to the right.

b.   Price level rises and real output rises.

c.   Price level rises and real output stays the same.

d.   No. Over time, people and firms adjust to the new higher amount of spending by raising prices and wages.

4. a. Short-run aggregate supply shifts left.

    b. Prices rise and output falls.

    c. stagflation

    d. Shift aggregate demand to the right.

    e. Prices would rise and remain there.

    f. The high unemployment at the low level of output would put pressure on the wage to fall back to its original value.

    g. No. Increases in the cost of production need to be "accommodated" by government policy in order to permanently raise prices.

5. a. Some firms mistakenly believe that only the price of their product has fallen and they cut back on production. As they realize that all prices are falling, they will increase production at each price, which will shift short-run aggregate supply to the right.

    b. Nominal wage contracts are based on the expectation of a higher price level; therefore, the real wage has risen and workers were laid off. As workers and firms recognize the fall in the price level, new contracts will have a lower nominal wage, the real wage falls, and firms increase production at each price level, thus shifting the short-run aggregate supply to the right.

    c. Some firms have not reduced their prices because of menu costs. Their products are relatively more expensive and sales fall. When they realize the lower price level is permanent, they lower their prices and production rises at each price level, thus shifting the short-run aggregate supply to the right.

    d. They would take place more slowly from a recession because the adjustment requires that prices and wages be reduced, and they are usually stickier downward. The adjustment when output is above the natural rate requires that prices and wages rise.

E. Advanced Critical Thinking

1. Yes. An increase in price expectations shifts the short-run aggregate-supply curve to the left, and prices rise.

2. No. In the long run, the increase in unemployment will cause wages and price expectations to fall back to their prior levels.

3. Yes. If policymakers accommodate the adverse supply shock with an increase in aggregate demand, the price level will rise permanently.

CHAPTER 15 The Influence of Monetary and Fiscal Policy on Aggregate Demand

I. Chapter Overview

A. Context and Purpose

Chapter 15 is the second chapter in a three-chapter sequence that concentrates on short-run fluctuations in the economy around its long-run trend. Chapter 14 introduced the model of aggregate supply and aggregate demand. Chapter 15 discusses how the government's monetary and fiscal policies affect aggregate demand. Chapter 16 explains some of the tradeoffs that occur between short-run and long-run objectives when the relationship between inflation and unemployment is addressed.

The purpose of Chapter 15 is to address the short-run effects of monetary and fiscal policies. Chapter 14 explained that when aggregate demand or short-run aggregate supply shifts, it causes fluctuations in output. As a result, policymakers sometimes try to offset these fluctuations in output by shifting aggregate demand with monetary and fiscal policy. Chapter 15 addresses the theory behind these policies and some of the shortcomings of stabilization policy.

B. Helpful Hints

1. *Activist stabilization policy has many descriptive names.* Activist stabilization policy is the use of discretionary monetary and fiscal policies to manage aggregate demand in such a way as to minimize fluctuations in output and to maintain output at the long-run natural rate. As such, activist stabilization policy is sometimes called *discretionary policy* to distinguish it from automatic stabilizers. It is also called *aggregate-demand management* because monetary and fiscal policies are used to adjust or manage total spending in the economy. Finally, because policymakers attempt to counter the business cycle by reducing aggregate demand when it is too high, and by increasing aggregate demand when it is too low, stabilization policy is sometimes referred to as *countercyclical policy*.

2. *Activist stabilization policy can be used to move output toward the long-run natural rate from levels of output that are either above or below the natural rate of output.* The examples of stabilization policy in the text assume the economy is in a recession—a period when output is below the long-run natural rate. However, activist stabilization policy can be used to reduce aggregate demand and output in periods when output exceeds the long-run natural rate. When output exceeds the natural rate of output, we sometimes say that the economy is in a boom or an expansion, or that the economy is overheating because, left alone, the economy will adjust to a higher level of expected prices and wages, and output will fall to

the natural rate of output (short-run aggregate supply shifts left). Most economists believe that the Bank of Canada needs political independence to combat an overheating economy. This is because the activist policy prescription for an overheating economy is a reduction in aggregate demand, which may encounter some political opposition. That is, "taking away the punch bowl just as the party gets going" is not likely to be politically popular.

3. *An important distinction between expansionary fiscal policy and monetary policy is the effect on interest rates in the short run.* An expansionary monetary policy (an increase in the money supply) lowers interest rates, which stimulates investment spending and shifts aggregate demand to the right. An expansionary fiscal policy (higher government spending or lower taxes) raises interest rates, which "crowds out" investment spending and partially reverses the initial increase in aggregate demand.

4. *In the long run in an open economy, Canada's interest rate must equal the world interest rate.* Under a flexible exchange rate, expansionary monetary policy causes the real exchange rate to depreciate, thus further stimulating aggregate demand. The rise in output and income increases money demand enough to lift Canada's interest rate up to the world interest rate. Expansionary fiscal policy causes the real exchange rate to appreciate, which depresses aggregate demand. The fall in output and income decreases money demand enough to drop Canada's interest rate down to the world interest rate.

5. *Under a fixed exchange rate, monetary policy is ineffective.* Under a fixed exchange rate, the Bank of Canada's responsibility to fix the external value of the Canadian dollar forces the Bank to intervene in the foreign exchange market, which means that it loses control of the money supply. Fiscal policy is effective only under a fixed exchange rate; it has no crowding-out effects on investment or net exports, and thus has a lasting effect on aggregate demand.

II. Self-Testing Challenges

A. True/False Questions

_____1.   An increase in the interest rate increases the quantity demanded of money because it increases the rate of return on money.

_____2.   When money demand is drawn on a graph with the interest rate on the vertical axis and the quantity of money on the horizontal axis, an increase in the price level shifts money demand to the right.

_____3.   Keynes's theory of liquidity preference suggests that the interest rate is determined by the supply and demand for money.

_____4.   Quantitative easing is when the central bank conducts open-market operations by buying corporate bonds and mortgage securities.

_____5.   An increase in the money supply shifts the money supply to the right, increases the interest rate, and decreases investment and consumption, which then shifts the aggregate-demand curve to the left.

_____6.   Suppose firms and consumers become pessimistic about the future and cut back on expenditures. If the Bank of Canada engages in activist stabilization policy, the policy response should be to decrease the money supply.

_____7.   The Bank of Canada cannot choose the size of the money supply and the external value of the Canadian dollar.

_____8.   Because of the multiplier effect, an increase in government spending of $4 billion will shift the aggregate-demand curve to the right by more than $4 billion (assuming there is no crowding out).

_____9.   If the *MPC* (marginal propensity to consume) is 0.80, then the value of the closed economy multiplier is 8.

_____10.   Crowding out occurs in a closed economy when an increase in government spending increases incomes, shifts money demand to the right, raises the interest rate, and reduces investment spending.

_____11.   A liquidity trap occurs when nominal interest rates are zero, and expansionary monetary policy has no effects on aggregate demand.

_____12.   Suppose firms and consumers become pessimistic about the future and cut back on expenditures. If fiscal policymakers engage in activist stabilization policy, the policy response should be to decrease government spending and increase taxes.

_____13.   Many economists prefer automatic stabilizers because they affect the economy with a shorter lag than activist stabilization policies.

_____14.   In the short run, the interest rate is determined by money demand and money supply in a closed economy, but not in an open economy.

_____15.   Employment Insurance benefits are an example of an automatic stabilizer because when incomes fall, Employment Insurance benefits rise.

B. Multiple-Choice Questions

1. Which one of the following determines the interest rate, as suggested by Keynes's liquidity preference theory of the interest rate?
   a. the supply and demand of loanable funds
   b. the supply and demand of money
   c. the supply and demand of labour
   d. aggregate supply and aggregate demand

2. When money demand is expressed in a graph with the interest rate on the vertical axis and the quantity of money on the horizontal axis, which one of the following is an outcome of an increase in the interest rate?
   a. The demand for money is decreased.
   b. The demand for money is increased.
   c. The quantity demanded of money is decreased.
   d. The quantity demanded of money is increased.

3. When the supply and demand for money are expressed in a graph with the interest rate on the vertical axis and the quantity of money on the horizontal axis, which one of the following is an outcome of an increase in the price level?
   a. Money demand is shifted to the right, and the interest rate is increased.
   b. Money demand is shifted to the left, and the interest rate is increased.
   c. Money demand is shifted to the right, and the interest rate is decreased.
   d. Money demand is shifted to the left, and the interest rate is decreased.

4. Which one of the following is the **MOST** important reason for the downward slope of the aggregate-demand curve in a closed economy?
   a. the fiscal effect
   b. the wealth effect
   c. the interest-rate effect
   d. the real exchange-rate effect

5. In the market for real output, which one of the following is the initial effect of an increase in the money supply?
   a. Aggregate demand shifts to the right.
   b. Aggregate demand shifts to the left.
   c. Aggregate supply shifts to the right.
   d. Aggregate supply shifts to the left.

6. Which one of the following is the short-run effect of an increase in the money supply in an open economy?
   a. an increase in the exchange rate
   b. a decrease in the price level
   c. an increase in the interest rate
   d. a decrease in the interest rate

7.   Which one of the following is the long-run effect of an increase in the money supply in an open economy?
   a.   It is greater under a flexible exchange rate.
   b.   It is smaller than in a closed economy.
   c.   It is greater under a fixed exchange rate.
   d.   It is the same as in a closed economy.

8.   Suppose a wave of business and consumer pessimism causes a reduction in spending. Which one of the following is the likely result if the Bank of Canada chooses to engage in activist stabilization policy?
   a.   It should increase government spending and decrease taxes.
   b.   It should decrease government spending and increase taxes.
   c.   It should increase the money supply and decrease interest rates.
   d.   It should decrease the money supply and increase interest rates.

9.   Which one of the following is an outcome of a decrease in government spending?
   a.   Aggregate supply is shifted to the right.
   b.   Aggregate supply is shifted to the left.
   c.   Aggregate demand is shifted to the right.
   d.   Aggregate demand is shifted to the left.

10.   If the marginal propensity to consume (MPC) is 0.80, and the marginal propensity to import (MPI) is 0.20, which one of the following is the value of the multiplier?
   a.   1.00
   b.   1.25
   c.   2.50
   d.   5.00

11.   Which one of the following would occur with an increase in the marginal propensity to consume (MPC)?
   a.   raised value of the multiplier
   b.   lowered value of the multiplier
   c.   no impact on the value of the multiplier
   d.   rarely any occurrence because the MPC is set by federal law

12.   Suppose a wave of business and consumer optimism has increased spending such that the current level of output exceeds the long-run natural rate. Which one of the following describes what action policymakers should take in order to engage in activist stabilization policy?
   a.   decrease taxes, which shifts aggregate demand to the right
   b.   decrease taxes, which shifts aggregate demand to the left
   c.   decrease government spending, which shifts aggregate demand to the right
   d.   decrease government spending, which shifts aggregate demand to the left

13.   Which one of the following terms refers to a scenario in which an increase in government spending in the short run raises incomes, shifts money demand to the right, raises the interest rate, and lowers investment?
a. the multiplier effect
b. the investment accelerator
c. the crowding-out effect
d. supply-side economics

14.   Which one of the following statements regarding taxes is correct?
a. A decrease in taxes shifts the aggregate-supply curve to the left.
b. An increase in taxes shifts the aggregate-demand curve to the right.
c. A change in taxes has a greater effect on aggregate demand under a fixed exchange rate than under a flexible exchange rate.
d. Most economists believe that, in the short run, the greatest impact of a change in taxes is on aggregate supply, not aggregate demand.

15.   Suppose that a recession in the United States decreases the demand for Canada's exports by $15 billion. Suppose that the *MPC* is 0.75 and the *MPI* is 0.25. Which one of the following is the most likely outcome?
a. The aggregate-demand curve shifts to the right by $15 billion.
b. The aggregate-demand curve shifts to the left by $15 billion.
c. The aggregate-demand curve shifts to the right by $30 billion.
d. The aggregate-demand curve shifts to the left by $30 billion.

16.   Which one of the following terms refers to an increase in government spending that increases the income of some people, such that those people would spend some of that increased income on additional consumer goods?
a. the multiplier effect
b. the investment accelerator
c. the crowding-out effect
d. supply-side economics

17.   Which one of the following terms refers to an increase in government spending that would cause firms to purchase additional plants and equipment?
a. the multiplier effect
b. the investment accelerator
c. the crowding-out effect
d. supply-side economics

18.   Which one of the following is an automatic stabilizer?
a. military spending
b. spending on public schools
c. Employment Insurance benefits
d. spending on civil service salaries

19.   Which one of the following statements about stabilization policy is true?
    a.   Parliament has no role in the use of fiscal policy.
    b.   Long lags enhance the ability of policymakers to "fine-tune" the economy.
    c.   Many economists prefer automatic stabilizers because they affect the economy with a shorter lag than does an activist stabilization policy.
    d.   In the short run, a decision by the Bank of Canada to increase the money supply is essentially the same as a decision to increase the interest rate.

20.   Which one of the following statements is correct?
    a.   Fiscal policy has no lasting impact on aggregate demand under a flexible exchange rate.
    b.   A flexible exchange rate eliminates the crowding-out effect on investment and net exports of an expansionary fiscal policy.
    c.   The Coyne Affair illustrated the conflict between the federal and provincial governments regarding the coordinated use of fiscal policy.
    d.   Keynes's book, *The General Theory of Employment, Interest, and Money*, emphasized the key role of aggregate supply in explaining short-run economic fluctuations.

C. Short-Answer Questions

1.   Why is the money-supply curve vertical when it is drawn on a graph with the interest rate on the vertical axis and the quantity of money on the horizontal axis?

    _____

    _____

2.   Why does the money-demand curve slope negatively when it is drawn on a graph with the interest rate on the vertical axis and the quantity of money on the horizontal axis? _____

    _____

    _____

    _____

3.   Explain the response of Canadian policymakers to the 2008–2009 recession.

    _____

    _____

    _____

    _____

    _____

4.   Explain how an increase in the money supply shifts the aggregate-demand curve in the short run. _____

    _____

    _____

    _____

5.   Explain the intuition of the multiplier effect resulting from an increase in government spending in a closed economy. Why should a bigger *MPC* make the multiplier effect larger? _____

_____

_____

_____

_____

6.   Explain how an increase in government spending may lead to crowding out in an open economy. _____

_____

_____

_____

_____

7.   What concept does the Coyne Affair of 1961 illustrate? _____

_____

_____

_____

_____

8.   How does a cut in taxes affect aggregate supply? _____

_____

_____

_____

_____

9.   Which is likely to have a greater impact on aggregate demand, a decrease in taxes with a flexible or a fixed exchange rate? Why? _____

_____

_____

_____

_____

10.   Explain why taxes and government spending may act as automatic stabilizers.

_____

_____

_____

_____

D. Practice Problems

1. Three cases are listed below. If the Bank of Canada was to engage in activist stabilization policy, in which direction should it move the money supply in response to each case?

   a. A wave of optimism boosts business investment and household consumption.

   _____

   _____

   b. OPEC raises the price of crude oil.

   _____

   _____

   c. Foreigners reduce their demand for Canadian lumber.

   _____

   _____

2. Three cases are listed below. If the Minister of Finance was to use fiscal policy to actively stabilize the economy, in which direction should government spending and taxes change in response to each case?

   a. A wave of pessimism reduces business investment and household consumption. _____

   _____

   b. Foreigners increase their demand for Canadian-produced telecommunications equipment. _____

   _____

   c. The world price of crude oil falls._____

   _____

3. Suppose the economy is in a recession. Policymakers estimate that aggregate demand is $30 billion short of the amount necessary to generate the long-run natural rate of output. That is, if aggregate demand were shifted to the right by $30 billion, the economy would be in long-run equilibrium.

   a. If the federal government chooses to use fiscal policy to stabilize the economy, by how much should they increase government spending if the marginal propensity to consume (MPC) is 0.90, the economy is closed, and there is no crowding out? _____

   _____

   _____

   _____

   _____

b. If the federal government chooses to use fiscal policy to stabilize the economy, by how much should they increase government spending if the marginal propensity to consume (*MPC*) is 0.90, the marginal propensity to import (*MPI*) in the open economy is 0.15, and there is no crowding out?

_____

_____

_____

c. If there is crowding out of investment spending in a closed economy, will the government need to spend more or less than the amount you found in (a) above? Why? _____

_____

_____

d. If investment spending by firms in a closed economy is very sensitive to changes in the interest rate, is crowding out more of a problem or less of a problem? Why? _____

_____

_____

_____

e. If policymakers discover that the lag for fiscal policy in a closed economy is two years, should that make them more likely to employ fiscal policy as a stabilization tool, or more likely to allow the economy to adjust on its own? Why? _____

_____

_____

_____

4. a. What does an increase in the money supply do to interest rates in an open economy in the short run? Explain. _____

_____

_____

_____

b. What does an increase in the money supply do to interest rates in an open economy in the long run? Explain. _____

_____

_____

_____

c. Are these results inconsistent? Explain. _____

_____

_____

_____

E. Advanced Critical Thinking

You are watching a nightly network news broadcast. The business correspondent reports that the Bank of Canada raised interest rates by a quarter of a percent today to head off future inflation. The report then moves to interviews with prominent politicians. The response of the leader of the official opposition is negative. She says, "The Consumer Price Index has not increased, yet the Bank of Canada is restricting growth in the economy, supposedly to fight inflation. My constituents will want to know why they are going to have to pay more when they get a loan, and I do not have a good answer. I think this is an outrage and I think Parliament should have hearings on the Bank of Canada's policymaking powers."

1. What interest rate did the Bank of Canada raise?

   _____

2. State the Bank of Canada's policy in terms of the money supply.

   _____

   _____

3. Why might the Bank of Canada raise interest rates before the CPI starts to rise?

   _____

   _____

   _____

4. Use the opposition politician's statement to explain why **MOST** economists believe that the Bank of Canada needs to be independent of politics.

   _____

   _____

   _____

III. Solutions

A. True/False Questions

1. F; an increase in the interest rate decreases the quantity demanded of money because it raises the opportunity cost of holding money.
2. T
3. T
4. T
5. F; an increase in the money supply decreases the interest rate, and increases investment and consumption, which shifts aggregate demand to the right.
6. F; the Bank of Canada should increase the money supply.
7. T
8. T
9. F; the value of the multiplier is 5.
10. T

11. T
12. F; policymakers should increase government spending and decrease taxes.
13. T
14. F; in the short run, the interest rate is determined by money demand and money supply in both open and closed economies.
15. T

B. Multiple-Choice Questions

1. b	5. a	9. d	13. c	17. b
2. c	6. d	10. c	14. c	18. c
3. a	7. a	11. a	15. d	19. c
4. c	8. c	12. d	16. a	20. a

C. Short-Answer Questions

1. The quantity of money is fixed at whatever level the Bank of Canada chooses, and this quantity is not dependent on the interest rate.

2. The interest rate is the opportunity cost of money because money earns no rate of return. Thus, an increase in the interest rate causes people to economize on cash balances and hold more wealth in interest-bearing bonds.

3. The Bank of Canada implemented an expansionary monetary policy while maintaining a flexible exchange rate. The Bank of Canada increased the money supply, lowered interest rates, and pushed the aggregate-demand curve to the right. The Minister of Finance implemented an expansionary fiscal policy of tax cuts and spending increases.

4. The money-supply curve shifts right, the interest rate decreases, and investment and consumption increase at each price level, which is a rightward shift in the aggregate-demand curve.

5. When the government purchases goods and services, it causes an increase in the incomes of the sellers. They spend some proportion of their new higher income on goods and services, raising others' incomes, and so on. The higher the *MPC*, the greater the proportion of new income spent in each round.

6. An increase in government spending raises incomes, shifts money demand right, raises the interest rate, and crowds out investment. With a flexible exchange rate, the Canadian dollar appreciates, which crowds out net exports.

7. The Coyne Affair illustrates the need for coordinated fiscal and monetary policy. At that time, the federal government was pursuing an expansionary fiscal policy, but the Bank of Canada was determined to maintain a flexible exchange rate, which made the fiscal policy ineffective.

8. It causes an increase in aggregate supply by increasing the incentive to work and to produce goods and services.

9. A decrease in taxes with a fixed exchange rate, because then fiscal policy has no crowding-out effect on investment or net exports.

10. Income tax collections fall during a recession, and government spending on social assistance benefits and Employment Insurance benefits rises. Both of these stimulate aggregate demand.

D. Practice Problems

1. a. Decrease the money supply.

    b. Increase the money supply.

    c. Increase the money supply.

2. a. Increase spending, decrease taxes.

    b. Decrease spending, increase taxes.

    c. Decrease spending, increase taxes.

3. a. Multiplier = $1/(1 - 0.90) = 10$; $30/10 = $3.0 billion

    b. Multiplier = $1/(1 - 0.90 + 0.15) = 4$; $30/4 = $7.5 billion

    c. More, because as the government spends more, firms spend less on plants and equipment, so aggregate demand will not increase by as much as the multiplier suggests.

    d. More of a problem. Government spending raises interest rates. The more sensitive investment is to the interest rate, the more it is reduced or crowded out by government spending.

    e. More likely to allow the economy to adjust on its own, because if the economy adjusts on its own before the impact of the fiscal policy is felt, the fiscal policy will be destabilizing.

4. a. It lowers interest rates. An increase in the money supply requires a decrease in interest rates to induce people to hold the additional money.

    b. It has no effect because, in the long run, Canada's interest rate must equal the world interest rate.

c. No. In the short run, interest rates adjust to balance the supply and demand for money. In the long run, Canada's interest rate equals the world interest rate, and net capital outflow adjusts to balance the supply and demand for loanable funds.

E. Advanced Critical Thinking

1. The overnight rate.

2. They decreased the money supply (or lowered its growth rate).

3. Monetary policy acts on the economy with a lag of at least six months. If the Bank of Canada waits until inflation has arrived, the effect of its policy will arrive too late. Thus, the Bank of Canada responds to its forecast of inflation.

4. Politicians must be responsive to the short-term needs of voters. Monetary policy must take a long-term view and make politically painful decisions when the economy is overheating (when output is above the long-run natural rate).

CHAPTER 16 The Short-Run Tradeoff between Inflation and Unemployment

I. Chapter Overview

A. Context and Purpose

Chapter 16 is the final chapter in a three-chapter sequence about the economy's short-run fluctuations in output around its long-run trend. Chapter 14 introduced aggregate supply and aggregate demand. Chapter 15 developed how monetary and fiscal policy affect aggregate demand. Both Chapters 14 and 15 addressed relationships between the price level and output. Chapter 16 will concentrate on a similar relationship between inflation and unemployment.

The purpose of Chapter 16 is to trace the history of economists' thinking about the relationship between inflation and unemployment. The chapter explains why there is a temporary tradeoff between inflation and unemployment, and why there is no permanent tradeoff. This result is an extension of the results produced by the model of aggregate supply and aggregate demand where a change in the price level caused by a change in aggregate demand temporarily alters output but has no permanent impact on output.

B. Helpful Hints

1. *Short-run and long-run Phillips curves are almost a mirror image of short-run and long-run aggregate-supply curves.* Look at Figures 16.2 and 16.4 of the text. Notice the aggregate-supply curves in panel (a). Compare them to the Phillips curves in panel (b). They appear to be mirror images of each other. The long-run aggregate-supply curve is vertical because, in the long run, an increase in the price level is met by a proportionate increase in all prices and incomes; therefore, no incentive to alter production exists. Because an increase in prices has no effect on output in the long run, it has no effect on unemployment, and the long-run Phillips curve is vertical in panel (b). In the short-run, with price expectations fixed, an increase in the price level provides an incentive for firms to increase production, which causes the short-run aggregate-supply curve to be positively sloped in panel (a). When output rises, unemployment tends to fall; therefore, the short-run Phillips curve is negatively sloped in panel (b). In summary, because both graphs employ some measure of prices on the vertical axis, and because each graph uses real measures of economic activity that are negatively correlated on their respective horizontal axes (an increase in output is associated with a decrease in unemployment), then aggregate-supply curves and Phillips curves should "mirror" each other.

2. *To understand the short-run Phillips curve, review the short-run aggregate-supply curve.* To gain confidence deriving and shifting short-run Phillips curves, review the sources to the positive slope of the short-run aggregate-supply curve in Chapter 14. Chapter 14 contains reminders that there are a number of reasons why a short-run aggregate-supply curve slopes positively: misperceptions about relative price, sticky wages, and sticky prices. Because short-run aggregate-supply curves and short-run Phillips curves are mirror images of each other, the reasons that produce a positive slope in short-run aggregate supply are the very same reasons that produce a negative slope in the short-run Phillips curve. Also, recall that all three theories of the short-run aggregate-supply curve are based on the assumption of fixed price expectations. When expected inflation rises, the short-run aggregate-supply curve shifts left. Correspondingly, because the short-run aggregate-supply curve and the short-run Phillips curve are mirror images, a rise in expected inflation shifts the short-run Phillips curve to the right.

3. *Estimates of the natural rate of unemployment vary widely, which causes policymakers to disagree on the appropriate monetary and fiscal policies.* When looking at a Phillips curve graph or the model of aggregate supply and aggregate demand, it appears as if policymakers should always know whether to expand or contract aggregate demand or whether to leave aggregate demand alone. This is because it can be seen whether the economy is operating above or below the natural rate of unemployment chosen on the graph. In reality, however, the natural rate of unemployment is very difficult to measure, and policymakers are uncertain whether the economy is actually operating above or below the natural rate of unemployment. For example, if the economy is currently operating at 6 percent unemployment, the economy is operating below capacity if the natural rate of unemployment is 5 percent; it is operating at capacity if the natural rate is 6 percent, and it is operating above capacity if the natural rate is 7 percent. Each situation might suggest a different stabilization policy, even though the actual rate of unemployment is unchanged at 6 percent.

II. Self-Testing Challenges

A. True/False Questions

_____1. The Phillips curve illustrates the positive relationship between inflation and unemployment.

_____2. If inflation is 3 percent and unemployment is 8 percent, the misery index is 5 percent.

_____3. In the short run, an increase in aggregate demand increases the price level and output, and decreases unemployment.

_____4. When unemployment is below the natural rate, the labour market is unusually tight, thus putting pressure on wages and prices to rise.

_____5.   An increase in expected inflation shifts the Phillips curve to the right and makes the inflation–unemployment tradeoff less favourable.

_____6.   An increase in the money supply increases inflation and permanently decreases unemployment.

_____7.   In the long run, the unemployment rate is independent of inflation and the Phillips curve is vertical at the natural rate of unemployment.

_____8.   When actual inflation exceeds expected inflation, unemployment exceeds the natural rate.

_____9.   The natural-rate hypothesis suggests that, in the long run, unemployment returns to its natural rate, regardless of inflation.

_____10.   An adverse supply shock, such as an increase in the price of imported oil, shifts the Phillips curve to the right and makes the inflation–unemployment tradeoff less favourable.

_____11.   One way that the Bank of Canada measures inflation expectations is through the Bank's Business Outlook Survey of Canadian firms.

_____12.   An increase in aggregate demand temporarily reduces unemployment, but after people raise their expectations of inflation, unemployment returns to the natural rate.

_____13.   In 1988, the Bank of Canada clearly and firmly stated its target of zero inflation. As a result, the sacrifice ratio was very small.

_____14.   If people have rational expectations, an announced monetary contraction by the Bank of Canada that is credible could reduce inflation with little or no increase in unemployment.

_____15.   If the sacrifice ratio is 5, to reduce inflation from 3 percent to 1 percent requires a reduction in output of 2 percent.

B. Multiple-Choice Questions

1. Which one of the following defines the misery index?
    a. It is the sum of the growth rate of output and the inflation rate.
    b. It is the sum of the unemployment rate and the inflation rate.
    c. It is the sum of the unemployment rate and the bank rate.
    d. It is the sum of the natural rate of unemployment and the actual rate of unemployment.

2. Which one of the following is illustrated by the original Phillips curve?
    a. the tradeoff between inflation and unemployment
    b. the positive relationship between inflation and unemployment
    c. the tradeoff between output and unemployment
    d. the positive relationship between output and unemployment

3. Which one of the following explains why the Phillips curve is an extension of the model of aggregate supply and aggregate demand?
    a. In the short run, an increase in aggregate demand increases the price level and decreases growth.
    b. In the short run, an increase in aggregate demand increases the price level and decreases inflation.
    c. In the short run, an increase in aggregate demand increases the price level and increases unemployment.
    d. In the short run, an increase in aggregate demand increases the price level and decreases unemployment.

4. Which of the following will be seen along a short-run Phillips curve?
    a. a higher rate of growth in output, associated with a lower inflation rate
    b. a higher rate of growth in output, associated with a higher unemployment rate
    c. a higher rate of inflation, associated with a lower unemployment rate
    d. a higher rate of inflation, associated with a higher unemployment rate

5. Suppose that, in the long run, people adjust their price expectations so that all prices and incomes move proportionately to an increase in the price level. Which one of the following describes the resultant long-run Phillips curve?
    a. It is vertical.
    b. It is negatively sloped.
    c. It is positively sloped.
    d. It has a slope that is determined by how fast people adjust their price expectations.

6. Suppose that, in the short run, policymakers choose an expansionary fiscal or monetary policy to lower the rate of unemployment. According to the Phillips curve, which one of the following will occur?
    a. The economy will experience a decrease in inflation.
    b. The economy will experience an increase in inflation.
    c. Inflation will be unaffected if price expectations are unchanging.

7. Which one of the following describes outcomes of an increase in expected inflation?
    a. The short-run Phillips curve shifts to the right, and the unemployment–inflation tradeoff becomes less favourable.
    b. The short-run Phillips curve shifts to the left, and the unemployment–inflation tradeoff becomes more favourable.
    c. The short-run Phillips curve shifts to the right, and the unemployment–inflation tradeoff becomes more favourable.
    d. The short-run Phillips curve shifts to the left, and the unemployment–inflation tradeoff becomes less favourable.

8. Which one of the following would shift the long-run Phillips curve to the left?
    a. a decrease in the price of imported oil
    b. a decrease in expected inflation
    c. a decrease in aggregate demand
    d. a reduction in Employment Insurance benefits

9. Which one of the following occurs if actual inflation exceeds expected inflation?
    a. Unemployment is greater than the natural rate of unemployment.
    b. Unemployment is less than the natural rate of unemployment.
    c. Unemployment is equal to the natural rate of unemployment.
    d. In the future, people will reduce their expectations of inflation.

10. Which one of the following describes outcomes of a decrease in the price of imported oil?
    a. The short-run Phillips curve shifts to the right, and the unemployment–inflation tradeoff becomes more favourable.
    b. The short-run Phillips curve shifts to the right, and the unemployment–inflation tradeoff becomes less favourable.
    c. The short-run Phillips curve shifts to the left, and the unemployment–inflation tradeoff becomes more favourable.
    d. The short-run Phillips curve shifts to the left, and the unemployment–inflation tradeoff becomes less favourable.

11. Which one of the following describes the argument of the natural-rate hypothesis?
    a. Unemployment is always above the natural rate.
    b. Unemployment is always below the natural rate.
    c. Unemployment is always equal to the natural rate.
    d. In the long run, the unemployment rate returns to the natural rate, regardless of inflation.

Use the following graph for questions 12–17.

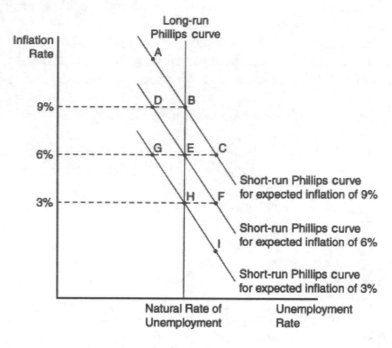

12.   Suppose that people in the economy expect inflation to be 3 percent, and inflation is actually 3 percent. According to the above graph, at which point is the economy operating?
    a.   F
    b.   G
    c.   H
    d.   I

13.   Suppose people in the economy expect inflation to be 6 percent, but inflation turns out to be 3 percent. According to the above graph, at which point is the economy operating?
    a.   D
    b.   E
    c.   F
    d.   H

14.   Suppose the economy is in long-run equilibrium at point E. A sudden increase in government spending occurs. According to the above graph, which one of the following is the direction that the economy should move?
    a.   in the direction of point A
    b.   in the direction of point B
    c.   in the direction of point C
    d.   in the direction of point D

15. Suppose the economy is operating at point D in the above graph. Which one of the following describes what will occur as people revise their inflation expectations?
   a. The long-run Phillips curve will shift to the left.
   b. The short-run Phillips curve will shift in the direction of the short-run Phillips curve for expected inflation of 3 percent.
   c. The short-run Phillips curve will shift in the direction of the short-run Phillips curve for expected inflation of 6 percent.
   d. The short-run Phillips curve will shift in the direction of the short-run Phillips curve for expected inflation of 9 percent.

16. Suppose the economy is operating in long-run equilibrium at point E. Which one of the following is the direction that the economy will move during an unexpected monetary contraction?
   a. C
   b. F
   c. G
   d. I

17. Suppose the economy is operating in long-run equilibrium at point E. A monetary contraction occurs. According to the above graph, which one of the following is the direction the economy should move in the long run?
   a. in the direction of point F
   b. in the direction of point G
   c. in the direction of point H
   d. in the direction of point I

18. If people have rational expectations, which one of the following could occur after a credible monetary policy contraction is announced?
   a. The announcement could reduce inflation with little or no increase in unemployment.
   b. The announcement could increase inflation with little or no decrease in unemployment.
   c. The announcement could increase inflation, but it would decrease unemployment by an unusually large amount.
   d. The announcement could reduce inflation, but it would increase unemployment by an unusually large amount.

19. If the sacrifice ratio is 3, which one of the following is required to reduce inflation from 5 percent to 2 percent?
   a. a reduction in output of 3 percent
   b. a reduction in output of 6 percent
   c. a reduction in output of 9 percent
   d. a reduction in output of 15 percent

20. Which one of the following would be the long-term result if the Bank of Canada were to continuously use expansionary monetary policy in an attempt to hold unemployment below the natural rate?
   a. an increase in the level of output
   b. a decrease in the unemployment rate
   c. an increase in the rate of inflation
   d. a decrease in the rate of inflation

C. Short-Answer Questions

1. How does the theory of rational expectations affect the size of the sacrifice ratio?

   _____

   _____

   _____

   _____

2. Use the model of aggregate demand and aggregate supply to describe why the short-run Phillips curve is negatively sloped. _____

   _____

   _____

   _____

3. Use the model of aggregate demand and aggregate supply to describe why the long-run Phillips curve is vertical. _____

   _____

   _____

   _____

   _____

4. Is the short-run Phillips curve actually a menu of inflation and unemployment combinations permanently available to the policymaker? Why or why not?

   _____

   _____

   _____

5. What is the natural-rate hypothesis? _____

   _____

   _____

   _____

6. If actual inflation exceeds expected inflation, is the unemployment rate above or below the natural rate? Why? _____

   _____

   _____

   _____

7. Which way does the short-run Phillips curve shift when there is an adverse aggregate-supply shock, such as an increase in the price of imported oil? Why?

_____

_____

_____

8. Referring to question 7 above, are the tradeoffs between unemployment and inflation that the economy now faces more favourable or less favourable than before the adverse aggregate-supply shock? Explain. _____

_____

_____

9. Referring to question 8 above, if the Bank of Canada accommodates the adverse aggregate-supply shock, what has the Bank revealed about the weights it attaches to the goals of low inflation and low unemployment? _____ _____

_____

10. What are two reasons why reducing inflation in the 1990s was so costly in terms of lost output? _____

_____

_____

_____

_____

_____

D. Practice Problems

1. Describe the initial effect of the following events on the short-run or long-run Phillips curve. That is, describe the movement along a given curve, or the direction of the shift in the curve.

a. An increase in expected inflation. _____

_____

b. An increase in the price of imported oil. _____

_____

c. An increase in the money supply. _____

_____

d. A decrease in government spending. _____

_____

e. A decrease in the minimum wage that lowers the natural rate of unemployment. _____

_____

2.   Use the Phillips curves in the following graph to answer the following questions.

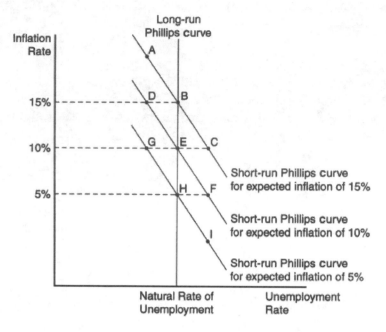

a. At what point is the economy located if people expect 10 percent inflation and inflation is actually 10 percent? _____

_____

b. Referring to question (a) above, is unemployment above, below, or equal to the natural rate? _____

_____

c. At what point is the economy located if people expect 10 percent inflation and the actual rate of inflation is 15 percent? _____

_____

d. Suppose the economy is operating at point D. Over time, in which direction will people revise their expectations of inflation: up or down?

_____

e. Suppose the economy is operating at point D. As people revise their expectations of inflation, in which direction will the short-run Phillips curve shift: right or left? _____

_____

f. Suppose the economy is operating at point E. In the short run, a sudden decrease in aggregate demand will move the economy toward which point?

_____

g. Suppose the economy is operating at point E. In the long run, a decrease in government spending will tend to move the economy toward which point?

_____

h. Suppose people expect 5 percent inflation. If inflation actually ends up being 10 percent, in which direction will unemployment move: above or below the natural rate? _____

_____

3. Assume the economy is initially in long-run equilibrium.

a. What happens to unemployment and inflation in the short run if the Bank of Canada increases the growth rate of the money supply?

_____

b. What happens to unemployment and inflation in the long run if the Bank of Canada increases the growth rate of the money supply?

_____

c. Can printing money keep unemployment below the natural rate? Explain.

_____

_____

d. What is the end result of a central bank repeatedly attempting to hold unemployment below the natural rate with expansionary monetary policy? Explain. _____

_____

_____

4. Suppose the economy is operating at the natural rate of unemployment with a high rate of inflation (point A in the following graph). Suppose the Bank of Canada announces a sudden monetary contraction to reduce inflation. Shown below are two possible paths the economy might take to adjust to the new lower rate of money growth. Choose the path that **BEST** depicts what might happen in each of the following cases, and explain your reasoning.

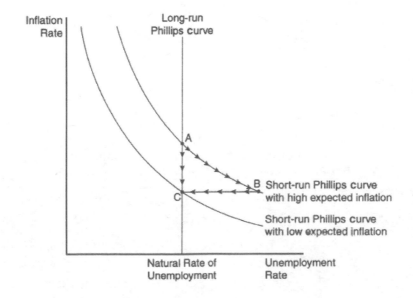

a. The Bank of Canada's announcement is not believed. _____

_____

_____

b. The Bank of Canada's announcement is believed and expectations of inflation are adjusted quickly. _____

_____

_____

c. The Bank of Canada's announcement is believed, but all workers have long-term wage contracts that cannot be renegotiated. _____

_____

_____

d. Which of the above cases (a, b, or c) **BEST** describes what would happen if, in the past, the Bank of Canada had repeatedly announced that inflation is its number one priority, but the Bank failed to actually engage in the threatened monetary contraction? Why? _____

_____

_____

E. Advanced Critical Thinking

A worldwide drought has reduced food production. Inflation has increased and unemployment has risen above the natural rate. Canadians are frustrated with their government. Some Canadians think, "This economic mess has got to be somebody's fault. A year ago, both inflation and unemployment were lower. We need to vote in some new politicians who know how to get rid of this inflation and unemployment."

1. The stagflation present in the economy is the fault of whom? _____

_____

_____

2. Are the current inflation and unemployment choices facing the economy better or worse than before the supply shock? What has happened to the short-run Phillips curve? _____

_____

_____

3. If policymakers increase aggregate demand in response to the supply shock, in what direction will the economy move along the new short-run Phillips curve? What will happen to inflation and unemployment? _____

_____

_____

4. If policymakers decrease aggregate demand in response to the supply shock, in what direction will the economy move along the new short-run Phillips curve? What will happen to inflation and unemployment? _____

_____

_____

5. Is there a policy that can immediately reduce both inflation and unemployment? Explain. _____

_____

_____

III. Solutions

A. True/False Questions

1. F; the Phillips curve illustrates the negative relationship between inflation and unemployment.
2. F; the misery index is 11 percent.
3. T
4. T
5. T
6. F; an increase in the money supply may temporarily decrease unemployment.
7. T
8. F; when actual inflation exceeds expected inflation, unemployment is below the natural rate.
9. T
10. T
11. T
12. T
13. F; the sacrifice ratio increased to about 6, much higher than in the previous decade.
14. T
15. F; output must be reduced by $5 \times 2\% = 10\%$.

B. Multiple-Choice Questions

1. b	5. a	9. b	13. c	17. c
2. a	6. b	10. c	14. d	18. a
3. d	7. a	11. d	15. d	19. c
4. c	8. d	12. c	16. b	20. c

C. Short-Answer Questions

1.   If the central bank made a credible commitment to low inflation, people would be rational enough to lower their expectations of inflation immediately. The short-run Phillips curve would shift downwards, and the economy would achieve low inflation without any lost output.

2.   An increase in aggregate demand increases the price level and output along the short-run aggregate-supply curve, which reduces unemployment. Inflation has increased and unemployment has decreased.

3.   An increase in aggregate demand increases the price level, but output remains at the natural rate of output due to a vertical long-run aggregate-supply curve. Inflation has increased but unemployment remains at the natural rate of unemployment.

4.   No. When inflation increases above expected inflation, unemployment temporarily decreases. However, after people revise their price expectations upward, the Phillips curve shifts to the right.

5.   Unemployment returns to the natural rate in the long run, regardless of inflation.

6.   Below. If prices are higher than expected, more output is produced and more people are employed, thus reducing unemployment.

7.   Short-run aggregate supply shifts left, showing lower output at each price level. Thus the Phillips curve shifts right, showing more unemployment at each rate of inflation.

8.   Less favourable. Now, at each level of unemployment, inflation is higher; or at each rate of inflation, unemployment is higher.

9.   The Bank of Canada is more concerned with low unemployment.

10.   The budget deficits of the federal and provincial governments remained high over this period, causing people's expectations of inflation to remain high. Also, the federal government was forecasting 3 percent inflation in its budgets, causing people and firms to adjust their expectations of inflation above the Bank's inflation target.

D. Practice Problems

1.   a. Shifts short-run Phillips curve to the right.

      b. Shifts short-run Phillips curve to the right.

      c. Move up the short-run Phillips curve.

      d. Move down the short-run Phillips curve.

      e. Long-run Phillips curve shifts left.

2.   a. E

      b. equal to the natural rate

      c. D

      d. up

      e. right

      f. F

      g. H

      h. below the natural rate

3.   a. Inflation increases, unemployment decreases.

      b. Inflation increases, unemployment stays at the natural rate.

      c. No. Unemployment temporarily decreases, but as people grow to expect the higher inflation, unemployment returns to the natural rate.

      d. Continued attempts to move unemployment below the natural rate simply cause inflation.

4.   a. Economy moves from A to B because people fail to reduce their price expectations and wage demands, so unemployment rises as inflation falls.

      b. Economy moves from A to C because people reduce their prices and wages proportionately.

      c. Economy moves from A to B because people are unable to actually reduce some of their wages and prices, so unemployment rises as inflation falls.

d. Case (a). It is rational for people to distrust a policymaker that has been untruthful before.

E. Advanced Critical Thinking

1. No one. It was an act of nature.

2. Worse. The short-run Phillips curve has shifted to the right.

3. The economy moves upward along the new short-run Phillips curve. Unemployment will be reduced but inflation will be increased.

4. The economy moves downward along the new short-run Phillips curve. Inflation will be reduced but unemployment will be increased.

5. No, the economy faces tradeoffs in the short run. A policy that reduces inflation increases unemployment. A policy that reduces unemployment increases inflation.

I. Chapter Overview

A. Context and Purpose

Chapter 17 is the final chapter in the text. It addresses five unresolved issues in macroeconomics, each of which is central to current political debates. The chapter can be studied all at once, or portions of the chapter can be studied in conjunction with prior chapters that deal with the related material.

The purpose of Chapter 17 is to provide both sides of five leading debates over macroeconomic policy. It employs information and tools you have accumulated in your study of this text. This chapter may help you take a position on the issues addressed or, at least, it may help you understand the reasoning of others who have taken a position.

B. Helpful Hints

1. *A policy that destabilizes the economy moves the economy away from the natural rate of output.* Stabilization policy is the use of monetary and fiscal policy to help move the economy toward the natural rate of output. However, if policy lags are long and unpredictable, the economy may have adjusted back to the natural rate of output (from an aggregate-demand or an aggregate-supply shock) before the impact of the stabilization policy is felt. In this case, the stabilization policy would then move the economy away from the natural rate of output, and the policy would be considered destabilizing.

2. *A political business cycle tends to involve both a monetary expansion prior to an election and a monetary contraction after an election.* Political business cycles are discussed in the text with regard to the policymaker's behaviour prior to elections. That is, prior to an election, a monetary expansion could increase output and decrease unemployment, thus enhancing the probability of the incumbent party's re-election. However, because this will tend to cause inflation after the election, this type of abuse of power usually involves a monetary contraction after the election to reduce inflationary pressures. Thus, the economy would tend to fluctuate between good economic performance prior to an election and poor economic performance after an election.

3. *Most economists support a cyclically balanced budget.* Federal government spending and tax collections depend on the level of output. For example, when output is above the natural rate, Employment Insurance expenditures decrease and tax collections increase, thus moving the budget toward surplus. When output is below the natural rate, Employment Insurance expenditures increase and tax

collections decrease, thus moving the budget toward deficit. Inflexible rules requiring a continuously balanced budget would require the government to reduce spending or raise taxes during recessions, and to raise government spending or cut taxes during economic booms, any of which would destabilize the economy further. Therefore, most economists suggest that the budget be balanced over the course of a business cycle—or what is termed a cyclically balanced budget—as opposed to a budget that is balanced each and every year.

II. Self-Testing Challenges

A. True/False Questions

_____1.   Monetary policy affects the economy with a lag, but fiscal policy has no lag.

_____2.   Monetary policy may suffer from time inconsistency because policymakers have an incentive to engage in a policy that differs from their policy announcements.

_____3.   The political business cycle refers to a situation in which corporate executives also hold political office.

_____4.   Opponents of an independent central bank argue that monetary policy is not an effective tool for influencing voters.

_____5.   Supporters of a zero-inflation target for monetary policy argue that the cost of reducing inflation is temporary, while the benefits of reducing inflation are permanent.

_____6.   Those opposed to a zero-inflation target for monetary policy argue that some of the costs of inflation can be eliminated by inflation-indexed income tax brackets and bonds.

_____7.   Government debt tends to redistribute wealth from the current generation to future generations.

_____8.   The federal government's debt should be evaluated by taking into account inflation, population growth, and income growth.

_____9.   Replacing the income tax with a consumption tax may increase saving, but it will tend to benefit the rich more than the poor.

_____10.   A reduction in the taxes on interest income will increase saving if the substitution effect from the increase in after-tax interest outweighs the income effect.

B. Multiple-Choice Questions

1. Suppose that the economy is suffering from pessimism on the part of consumers and firms. Which one of the following is an activist stabilization policy that "leans against the wind"?
    a. Policymakers should increase the money supply.
    b. Policymakers should increase taxes.
    c. Policymakers should increase interest rates.
    d. Policymakers should decrease government spending.

2. Which one of the following would be stated by an economist who argues that policymakers **should** try to stabilize the economy?
    a. The first rule of policymaking should be, "Do no harm."
    b. Stabilization policy can effectively reduce the large booms and busts of the business cycle.
    c. Because forecasting shocks to the economy is difficult, well-intended policy could be destabilizing.
    d. Because stabilization policy affects the economy with a lag, well-intended policy could be destabilizing.

3. Which one of the following terms refers to fluctuations in the economy caused by politicians' manipulation of the economy for the purpose of affecting electoral outcomes?
    a. the substitution effect
    b. the discretionary effect
    c. the political business cycle
    d. the time inconsistency of policy

4. Which one of the following terms refers to the discrepancy between policy announcements and policy actions?
    a. the substitution effect
    b. the discretionary effect
    c. the political business cycle
    d. the time inconsistency of policy

5. Which one of the following statements would be made by an economist who argues that monetary policy should be made by an independent central bank?
    a. The sacrifice ratio will be higher.
    b. It leads to a higher rate of inflation in the long run.
    c. It increases accountability for monetary policy choices.
    d. Empirical evidence shows that countries with the most independent central bank tend to have the lowest rates of inflation.

6.   Which one of the following is an example of an activist policy action that further destabilizes the economy?
    a. Firms become pessimistic and the Bank of Canada responds with a reduction in interest rates.
    b. Consumers become pessimistic and fiscal policymakers respond with a reduction in taxes.
    c. Firms become excessively optimistic and the Bank of Canada responds with a reduction in the money supply.
    d. Consumers become pessimistic and fiscal policymakers respond with a reduction in government spending.

7.   Which one of the following arguments would be made by an economist who does **NOT** support a zero-inflation target for monetary policy?
    a. Inflation imposes costs on the economy, such as shoeleather costs and menu costs.
    b. The cost of reducing inflation to zero is temporary, while the benefits are permanent.
    c. The cost of reducing inflation to zero is always reduced if a zero-inflation policy is credible.
    d. Zero inflation allows for the possibility of negative real interest rates.

8.   Which one of the following tends to be an effect of government debt?
    a. redistribution of wealth from future generations to the current generation
    b. redistribution of wealth from the current generation to future generations
    c. no redistributive effects

9.   Which one of the following is true with respect to government budget deficits?
    a. Budget deficits increase national saving.
    b. Budget deficits lead to lower taxes on future taxpayers.
    c. Budget deficits are the only way to transfer income across generations of taxpayers.
    d. Budget deficits reduce capital investment, future productivity, and, therefore, future incomes.

10.   Which one of the following would be argued by an economist who believes that the central bank should **NOT** aim for zero inflation?
    a. Those who lose their jobs often have the most skills and experience.
    b. The cost of reducing inflation is spread equitably over the population.
    c. The social costs of disinflation are larger than the economic costs of disinflation.
    d. Inflation makes it more difficult for real wages to adjust to changes in labour market conditions.

11. Which one of the following statements would be made by an economist who argues that the government should balance its budget?
    a. The government debt per person is relatively small compared to a person's lifetime earnings.
    b. Budget deficits lower the living standards of future generations.
    c. If parents save more and leave a larger bequest, there is no intergenerational redistribution of wealth from budget deficits.
    d. Budget deficits will not become an increasing burden as long as the debt does not grow more quickly than a nation's nominal income.

12. Which one of the following changes to tax laws would encourage more saving but also increase the relative tax burden on low-income people?
    a. Increase taxes on the return to saving.
    b. Decrease the GST from 5 percent to 3 percent, while raising personal income tax rates.
    c. Increase the maximum amount that households can contribute to an RRSP or a TFSA.

13. Which one of the following describes the conditions under which a reduction in taxes that increases the after-tax return to saving will in turn increase the quantity of saving in the economy?
    a. if the policy is time inconsistent
    b. if the income effect from the increase in after-tax return to saving equals the substitution effect
    c. if the income effect from the increase in after-tax return to saving exceeds the substitution effect
    d. if the substitution effect from the increase in after-tax return to saving exceeds the income effect

14. Which one of the following tends to be an outcome of tax reform that encourages saving?
    a. The budget deficit is reduced.
    b. The rate of growth of output is reduced.
    c. The tax burden is shifted toward high-income people and away from low-income people.
    d. The tax burden is shifted toward low-income people and away from high-income people.

15. Which one of the following occurs if monetary policy is time inconsistent?
    a. The short-run Phillips curve shifts upward.
    b. The short-run Phillips curve shifts downward
    c. The long-run Phillips curve shifts to the right.
    d. The long-run Phillips curve shifts to the left.

C. Short-Answer Questions

1. Why would an improvement in ability to forecast shocks to the economy improve use of activist stabilization policy? _____

_____

_____

2. What is the difference between inflation targeting and price level targeting?

_____

_____

_____

_____

_____

_____

_____

3. Why are the costs of inflation permanent but the costs of reducing inflation temporary? _____

_____

_____

_____

4. What could the federal government do to reduce some of the costs of continuous inflation? _____

_____

5. In what two ways does the government debt harm future generations?

_____

_____

6. Does a balanced federal government budget eliminate all redistributions of wealth across generations? Explain. _____

_____

_____

_____

_____

_____

7. For an increase in the after-tax return to saving to cause an increase in saving, which effect must outweigh the other: the substitution effect or the income effect? Why? _____

_____

_____

_____

_____

_____

8. Why will reforming tax laws to encourage saving tend to increase the tax burden on the poor? _____

_____

_____

_____

_____

D. Practice Problems

1. Suppose a wave of pessimism engulfs consumers and firms and causes them to reduce their expenditures.

   a. Demonstrate this event with the model of aggregate demand and aggregate supply. Assume that the economy was originally in long-run equilibrium.

   b. What is the appropriate activist policy response for monetary and fiscal policy? In which direction would the activist policy shift aggregate demand?

   _____

   _____

   _____

   c. Suppose the economy can adjust on its own from the recession described in part (a) in one year. Suppose policymakers choose to use fiscal policy to stabilize the economy, but the political battle over taxes and spending takes more than one year. Demonstrate these events with the model of aggregate demand and aggregate supply.

d. Describe the sequence of events shown in the graph created in part (c) above. _____

_____

_____

_____

_____

e. Did the activist fiscal policy stabilize or destabilize the economy? Explain.

_____

_____

_____

2. Suppose the Bank of Canada repeatedly announces that it desires price stability, and that it is aiming for zero inflation; however, it consistently generates 3 percent inflation.

a. Will this type of behaviour on the part of the Bank of Canada reduce unemployment below the natural rate of unemployment in the long run? Why or why not? _____

_____

_____

b. Once people have formed expectations of 3 percent inflation, what would happen in the short run if the Bank of Canada actually did achieve zero inflation? _____

_____

_____

c. Would it help if Parliament passed a law requiring the Bank of Canada to target zero inflation? Why or why not? _____

_____

_____

E. Advanced Critical Thinking

Those opposed to government budget deficits argue, among other things, that budget deficits redistribute wealth across generations by allowing the current generation to enjoy the benefits of government spending, while future generations must pay for it.

1. Under which of the following two cases would a person argue that there is a greater intergenerational transfer of wealth? Why? _____

   _____

   _____

   _____

   _____

   Case a
   The government increases spending on social programs by buying apples and oranges for the poor, but the government refuses to raise taxes, thereby increasing the budget deficit.

   Case b
   The government increases spending on bridges, roads, and buildings, but the government refuses to raise taxes, thereby increasing the budget deficit.

2. Does the preceding example provide a method by which it might be judged when a deficit is fair to each generation and when it is not? Explain. _____

   _____

   _____

   _____

3. Why might this method be difficult to enforce in practice? _____

   _____

   _____

III. Solutions

A. True/False Questions

1. F; fiscal policy has a long lag due to the political process.
2. T
3. F; a political business cycle results when politicians manipulate the economy to improve their chance of re-election.
4. T
5. T
6. T
7. F; government debt redistributes wealth to the current generation from future generations.
8. T

9. T
10. T

B. Multiple-Choice Questions

1. a	5. d	9. d	13. d
2. b	6. d	10. c	14. d
3. c	7. d	11. b	15. a
4. d	8. a	12. c	

C. Short-Answer Questions

1. Macroeconomic shocks need to be forecast months or years into the future because there are lags in the implementation of activist stabilization policy.

2. The Bank of Canada's inflation target is 2 percent inflation. When actual inflation exceeds 2 percent, the Bank of Canada tightens monetary policy to lower the rate of inflation closer to the target. With a price level target, the Bank of Canada would target a certain price level in the future. For example, if the price level is 100 today, the Bank of Canada may target a price level of 120 ten years from now. With a price level target, inflation will need to speed up or slow down in order to hit the target.

3. Inflation imposes continuous costs on the economy, such as shoeleather costs and menu costs. Reducing inflation to zero will increase unemployment only temporarily, but it will eliminate the continuous costs of inflation.

4. Index the income tax brackets and issue inflation-indexed bonds.

5. It increases future taxes and lowers future incomes by reducing the capital stock.

6. No. Redistributions of wealth across generations can be caused by many different government policies. For example, an increase in Canada Pension Plan benefits paid to the current recipients would be financed by an increase in Canada Pension Plan payroll taxes on current workers. As a result, income is transferred from working people to retired people, yet the budget deficit is unaffected.

7. The substitution effect must outweigh the income effect. An increase in after-tax interest causes people to save more as people substitute saving for current consumption. However, the income effect of an increase in after-tax interest causes people to reduce the amount of saving necessary to reach a targeted amount of future consumption.

8. High-income people save more than low-income people; therefore, the income tax relief would go disproportionately to the rich. Also, to maintain tax revenue, consumption taxes might have to be raised, which would cause an additional burden on the poor.

D. Practice Problems

1. a.

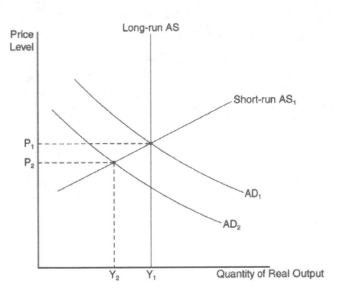

b. The appropriate response is to increase the money supply, lower interest rates, increase government spending, and/or decrease taxes. The activist policy would shift aggregate demand to the right.

c.

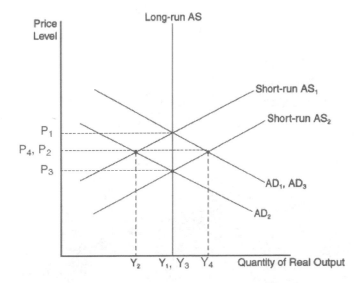

d. As short-run aggregate supply shifts to the right, the economy adjusts to the intersection of short-run AS_2 and AD_2. Then the expansionary aggregate-demand policy shifts aggregate demand to AD_3, and the economy moves to the intersection of short-run AS_2 and AD_3.

e. The activist policy destabilized the economy because the economy had already adjusted back to the natural rate of output; therefore, the increase in aggregate demand caused output to rise above the natural rate of output.

2. a. No. In the long run, people will grow to expect 3 percent inflation, and wages and prices will rise accordingly.

b. The economy would move down a short-run Phillips curve and inflation would fall, while unemployment would rise above the natural rate.

c. Yes. The Bank of Canada's announcement of a zero-inflation target would be more credible and the movement toward zero inflation would create a smaller increase in unemployment.

E. Advanced Critical Thinking

1. **Case a** has greater intergenerational transfer of wealth because the government purchased consumption goods that cannot be used by later generations, while in **Case b,** the government purchased physical capital that is durable and can be used by later generations.

2. It is more reasonable for the government to run a deficit and force future generations to pay for current expenditures if the expenditures are for capital goods that can be used by later generations.

3. Nearly every interest group can defend their spending as if it has a positive impact on future generations—military, education, etc.